WAL

SWALEDALE

HILLSIDE GUIDES - ACROSS THE NORTH

Circular Walks - Yorkshire Dales
• WHARFEDALE • MALHAMDALE • SWALEDALE • NIDDERDALE
• THREE PEAKS • WENSLEYDALE • HOWGILL FELLS
• HARROGATE & the WHARFE VALLEY • RIPON & LOWER WENSLEYDALE

Circular Walks - Lancashire and the North West
• BOWLAND • PENDLE & THE RIBBLE • LUNESDALE
• WEST PENNINE MOORS • ARNSIDE & SILVERDALE

Circular Walks - North Pennines
• TEESDALE • EDEN VALLEY • ALSTON & ALLENDALE

Circular Walks - North and East Yorkshire
• NORTH YORK MOORS, SOUTH • HOWARDIAN HILLS

Circular Walks - South Pennines
• ILKLEY MOOR • BRONTE COUNTRY
• CALDERDALE • SOUTHERN PENNINES

Hillwalking - Lake District
• LAKELAND FELLS - SOUTH • LAKELAND FELLS - EAST
• LAKELAND FELLS - NORTH • LAKELAND FELLS - WEST

Long Distance Walks
•COAST TO COAST WALK •DALES WAY •CUMBRIA WAY
•WESTMORLAND WAY •FURNESS WAY •LADY ANNE'S WAY •PENDLE WAY
•BRONTE WAY •CALDERDALE WAY •NIDDERDALE WAY

Short Scenic Walks - Full Colour Pocket Guides
•UPPER WHARFEDALE •LOWER WHARFEDALE •MALHAMDALE
•UPPER WENSLEYDALE •LOWER WENSLEYDALE •SWALEDALE
•NIDDERDALE •HARROGATE & KNARESBOROUGH
•RIBBLESDALE •AIRE VALLEY •ILKLEY & the WASHBURN VALLEY
•INGLETON & the WESTERN DALES •SEDBERGH & DENTDALE
•AMBLESIDE & LANGDALE •BORROWDALE
•BOWLAND •AROUND PENDLE •RIBBLE VALLEY

Send for a detailed current catalogue and price list
and also visit www.hillsidepublications.co.uk

WALKING COUNTRY

———

SWALEDALE

Paul Hannon

———

Hillside

HILLSIDE
PUBLICATIONS
20 Wheathead Crescent
Keighley
West Yorkshire
BD22 6LX

First published 1987
Fully Revised (10th) edition 2010

© Paul Hannon 1987, 2010

ISBN 978-1-907626-00-5

Cover illustration: Summer meadows near Keld
Back cover: Kisdon and the Swale Gorge;
Blakethwaite Smelt Mill, Gunnerside Gill; the Swale at Hoggarths
Page One: Kisdon Force
Page Three: Sundial, Keld
(Paul Hannon/Hillslides Picture Library)

The sketch maps in this book are based upon
1947 Ordnance Survey One-Inch maps
and earlier Six-Inch maps

Printed in Great Britain by
Carnmor Print
95-97 London Road
Preston
Lancashire
PR1 4BA

CONTENTS

WALKING COUNTRY - SWALEDALE

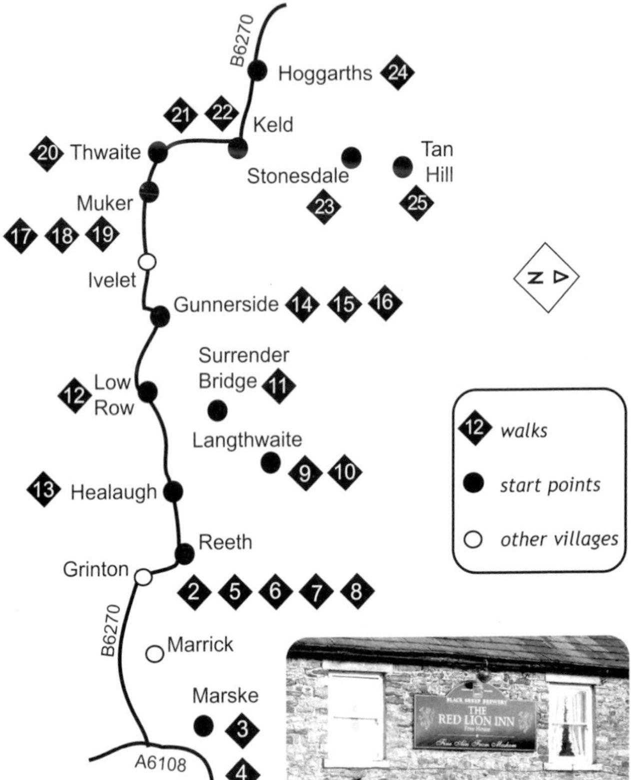

B6270

Hoggarths **24**

21 **22** Keld

20 Thwaite
Stonesdale

Tan Hill

Muker

23 **25**

17 **18** **19**

Ivelet

Gunnerside **14** **15** **16**

Surrender
Bridge **11**

12 Low Row

Langthwaite

9 **10**

13 Healaugh

Reeth

Grinton

2 **5** **6** **7** **8**

B6270

Marrick

Marske

3

A6108

4

RICHMOND **1**

N

12 walks

● start points

○ other villages

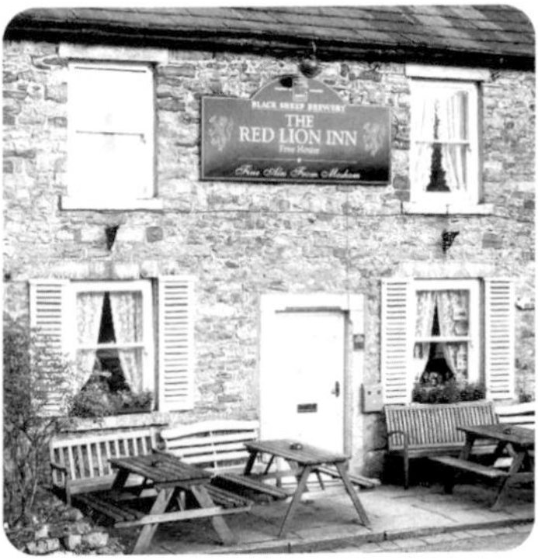

*The Red Lion Inn,
Langthwaite*

INTRODUCTION

The valley of the Swale is a very well defined one, from its beginnings in the tumbling becks of the wild Pennines to its elegant departure from the Yorkshire Dales National Park near Richmond. Swaledale is the most northerly of the Yorkshire Dales, and its remoteness from major centres of population has helped it remain relatively quiet and unchanged. With no disrespect to all of the other beautiful Dales valleys, it must be said that Swaledale is a bit special. The Swale is formed by the meeting of Great Sleddale and Birkdale Becks in the shadow of the high watershed west of Keld. Throughout its length the dale loses little grandeur, remaining steep-sided all the way to Richmond. The only sizeable tributary is Arkle Beck, which flows the length of Arkengarthdale to Reeth, and shares the characteristics of its parent valley. With its colourful, sweeping fellsides, there is more than a hint of Lakeland in Swaledale.

This is walkers' territory par excellence. The dale's attractions are largely of the natural variety, from heather moors to waterfalls, and inevitably back to the swift-flowing and often tree-lined river. You are in famous walking country in Swaledale: the Pennine Way crosses the valley head while the hugely popular Coast to Coast Walk treats its followers to the entire length of the dale, though largely avoids the river and thus most of the villages. And Swaledale's collection of idyllic villages is one of its finest assets: the higher dale settlements of Keld and Thwaite, Muker and Gunnerside are immensely characterful huddles of stone cottages, while all the valley's settlements nestle in a patchwork of meadows filled with archetypal field barns and parcelled up by a veritable maze of drystone walls.

There are two distinct types of walking in Swaledale, from the lush, flower-filled meadows to the remarkable mining-ravaged hillsides. These two aspects of the dale are its very trademark. No other valley in the park boasts such an unbroken line of riverbank footpaths, and no other has such an intense concentration of lead mining remains. Every corner of the dale seems to display evidence of the old industry, from the mines on the moors down through the gills with their smelt mills to the tiny villages with their miners' cottages. Many of the paths you follow lead to the sites of former workings, only slowly blending back into the hillsides. There is an impressiveness and a certain beauty about these places which stem partly from an image of those hardy souls who would walk several miles every day to toil in these dark, damp holes. The 19th century saw the industry peak, but also subsequently collapse largely due to the availability of cheaper foreign imports: sound familiar? As a result vast numbers of families left their native Swaledale for ever to ply their mining skills far across the oceans.

Earlier evidence of man is found on these hillsides too, with Iron Age earthworks seen at their most inspiring at Maiden Castle opposite Reeth. Hillside farming settlements such as Booze and West Stonesdale have changed little in centuries, while England's highest pub sits amid old coal mines at lonely Tan Hill. Swaledale's most impressive single historical feature is the imposing Norman

castle above the river at Richmond. This magnificent gateway to the valley is one of the finest little towns in the land, its medieval charm and character being a perfect match for the dale it guards. For those with transport it would make a reasonable base for the area, but Reeth, the largest village, is far more satisfactorily situated in walking terms with ample accommodation, numerous shops, pubs and cafes, and a beautiful setting.

A now vanished pub sign that recalls the influence of some of Swaledale's early settlers

Access to the countryside

The majority of walks in this guide are on public rights of way with no access restrictions. A handful also take advantage of the 2004 implementation of 'Right to Roam'. This freedom allows more logical routes to be created, and on most days of the year you are free to walk responsibly over these vast swathes of wonderful landscapes: such walks are noted in their introduction. Of various restrictions the two most notable are that dogs are normally banned from grouse moors; and also that the areas can be closed to walkers for up to 28 days each year, subject to advance notice being given. Inevitably the most likely times will be from the 'Glorious Twelfth', the start of the grouse shooting season in August. Further information can be obtained from the Countryside Agency (see page 95), and ideally from information centres. Finally, bear in mind that in springtime, avoiding tramping over open country away from paths and tracks would help to safeguard the most crucial period for vulnerable ground-nesting birds.

Getting around

Public transport to the area is largely limited to bus services to Richmond from Darlington, Northallerton and Leyburn. Nearest railway stations are at Kirkby Stephen to the west and Darlington to the east. Within the area, it couldn't be simpler: there is the Swaledale bus. This runs from Richmond up the dale to Keld, daily except Sundays. Utilising the Swaledale bus it is possible to link any number of these walks into linear routes, often creating a longer ramble, and at the same time keeping your car off the road.

Using the guide

Each walk is self contained, with essential information being followed by a concise route description and simple map. Dovetailed in between are notes and illustrations of features along the way. Snippets of information have been placed in *italics* to ensure that the essential route description is easier to locate. The sketch maps serve to identify the location of the routes rather than the fine detail, and whilst the description should be sufficient to guide you around, an Ordnance Survey map is strongly recommended.

To gain the most from a walk, the detail of the 1:25,000 scale Explorer maps is unsurpassed. It also gives the option to vary walks as desired, giving an improved picture of your surroundings and the availability of linking paths. One essential map covers all but one of the walks in this book:

• *Explorer OL30 - Yorkshire Dales North/Central*

• *Explorer 304 - Darlington & Richmond* covers the first walk only. Also useful for planning are Landranger maps 91, 92, 98 and 99.

1

WHITCLIFFE SCAR

START Richmond   Grid ref. NZ 157008

DISTANCE 5^3_4 miles (9km)

ORDNANCE SURVEY MAPS
1:50,000
Landranger 92 - Barnard Castle & Richmond
1:25,000
Explorer 304 - Darlington & Richmond

ACCESS Start from Round Howe car park on the Reeth road, on the edge of town a short mile west of the centre.

An airy promenade with spectacular views up the valley

Richmond is the gateway to Swaledale, although passing through it is the last thing to do. This is a truly remarkable town, steeped in history and dominated by the castle on its promontory high above the Swale. It was begun in 1071 by Alan Rufus, and the well preserved ruins are in the care of English Heritage and open to the public. Outstanding is the enormous 12th century keep, which watches over the whole town including, almost at its feet, the Market Place. This equally enormous feature shares double bill with the castle, and has a multitude of uses. In the centre of its sloping cobbles is the Holy Trinity church with its 14th century tower: it uniquely incorporates a row of shops, and houses the Green Howards Museum. Lined by shops and pubs the Market Place is used as a bus station as well as for its original purpose on Saturdays. A market cross is still very much in evidence. Outside of the square from which numerous wynds (narrow ways) radiate is St Mary's church, which includes a 14th century tower and 16th century stalls. Also in the vicinity is the impressive Grey Friars

Tower, across the road from the Georgian Theatre. This fascinating place dates from 1788, and having been restored in the 1960s it now serves its original function once more. The Culloden Tower stands nearer the river, which flows between two graceful bridges. Richmond has an information centre and even its own brewery. The presence of the military around the town is due to the proximity of Catterick Camp. Just downstream of the town stand the endearing remains of Easby Abbey, dating from 1152.

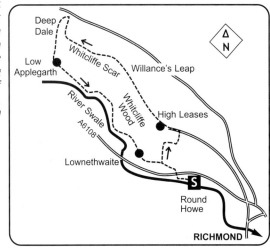

Monuments at Willance's Leap

The car park has WCs and a footbridge across the Swale: alongside is a caravan site. Take the path upstream from the car park, past picnic tables and into trees where it forks. *On the right is an old stone-arched culvert beneath the road.* Keep right, and just a few yards further take a path slanting right up to steps onto the main road. Cross and go left on a hedgerowed cart track. Before reaching a house turn sharp right up a more inviting hedge-rowed cart track making a splendid ascent. *The castle keep is seen over to the right.* It swings right to Low Leases then up again onto a surfaced access road. Go left, rising steadily past Whitcliffe Cottage then on a level course to High Leases on the left.

Pass through a gate above the house and leave the continuing track by a stile on the right, from where a grass path slants left up to a brow. Keeping to the higher, broader path well above a large gorse bank, this eases out and slants beneath an old field boundary and along to merge with a wall at the far corner. *Adjacent corner stiles to the left send a lower path along the inside of the wooded scar top, though it is initially somewhat overgrown.* Over the stile by the wall the right of way forks and immediately fades: bear left to the fence running along the wooded top of the eastern end of Whitcliffe Scar. *This long line of cliffs above a steep, wooded hill-side commands a superlative view of the lavishly wooded and steep-sided gorge which forms the portals to Swaledale.* This remains your course for some time, over an intervening stile and through a gateway before a better path forms to reach a pair of stiles at the corner of a tiny plantation. A path runs along the edge to a stile back out, and the adjoining wall leads quickly along to a kissing-gate in it at the monuments at Willance's Leap.

Marked by three monuments, an information panel and a seat, this recalls an incident in 1606 when Robert Willance's horse careered over the cliff, killing itself in the process but leaving its rider with only a broken leg. A good path heads on through scrub to a stile out into an open grassy bank, and keeps on with the wall above. As the massive cleft of Deep Dale intervenes, your level path swings round with it, still above the scar and then a farm road. Eventually the farm road is joined at its junction with a through road, and you double back left down it as far as a cattle-grid just short of High Applegarth. Take a stile just before it and descend right of a well-collapsed wall. The Coast to Coast Walk is crossed as you ignore its wall-stile to the left, dropping down to skirt the confines of Low Applegarth to a gate/stile in a fence. Just below it go left through a gateway, descending half-left through a gate/stile in a wall, and similarly through a larger pasture to join a fence on the left. Passing a ruined barn continue down to a stile and thence onto the riverbank opposite a caravan site.

Two lengthy riverside pastures ensue. The first is crossed on a sketchy way away the river, reaching a stile where the riverbank leads to a second stile. A second vast pasture is entered to begin a splendid section on the bank's lush turf above much evidence of erosion. A concession path permits you to simply trace the Swale all the way round to a gate at the far end. Here a track rises into trees to absorb the right of way path. The true right of way leaves the river quite soon, a broad green path heading away to a stile into the foot of Whitcliffe Wood. A clear path runs to the right to join the broad track used by the concession path. Together advance on, rising away from the river and up past a touching memorial to approach Lownethwaite at the end of the wood. The path avoids its confines by using a stile to cross the field bottom on the left, then joining a hedgerowed cart track to lead out to the main road, absorbing your outward route as you go. All that remains is to cross and drop back down to the car park.

Richmond Castle

GRINTON SMELT MILL

START Reeth   Grid ref. SE 038992

DISTANCE 6^{1}4 miles (10km)

ORDNANCE SURVEY MAPS
1:50,000
Landranger 98 - Wensleydale & Upper Wharfedale
1:25,000
Explorer OL30 - Yorkshire Dales, North/Central

ACCESS Start from the village centre. Roadside parking by the green. Served by bus from Richmond.

> *First-rate moorland ways either side of a splendid relic of the lead mining industry*

For a note on Reeth see WALK 6. Leave by the Richmond road at the bottom corner of the green, and along to Reeth Bridge. Soon after it bridges Arkle Beck take a kissing-gate on the right. The path runs between Fremington Mill Farm and the beck. *The building nearest you is the old mill itself, and the drained cut that supplied water from the beck is evident.* Beyond the farm the enclosed path emerges into a field: it short-cuts the beck's confluence with the Swale by veering left, on past a wall-corner to a kissing-gate and then straight ahead to steps up onto Grinton Bridge. Turn right over the bridge to the Bridge Inn on the corner. *The only settlement of any size on the south bank of the Swale, Grinton was once the major centre for the dale above Richmond. At the centre are pub, church, Literary Institute of 1903, and WCs. St Andrew's is known as the 'Cathedral of the Dales' because of its size. Until a chapel was established at Muker, Grinton parish extended through the entire valley as far as the Westmorland border. As this was the only consecrated ground prior to 1580, the deceased of the upper dale had to be borne a long and arduous journey known today as the 'corpse road'. Though of Norman origin, what you see is largely 15th century, being restored in the late 19th century.*

Leave by the side road climbing steeply past the church. It is quickly left by a little footbridge on the left alongside a driveway bridge. Pass between the houses (with a 1716 datestone on the right) to a stile into a field. Cross to the far end to one onto the road, but without setting foot on it take a stile alongside to ascend a wall-side. Through a gate at the top rise (crossing a water channel) to a stile alongside a stone shed. *Up above you is*

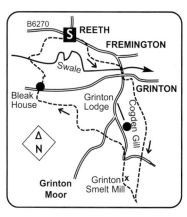

the castellated Grinton Lodge, built as a shooting lodge about 180 years ago and for many decades now a magnificently sited youth hostel. Already you enjoy big views back over the village to Reeth beneath Calver Hill. Here the path forks: ignore the stile ahead and slant left to the top corner of the field, crossing a small stream and a stile, then maintain this slant through two further fields to a stile onto the bracken flanks in front of Cogden Gill.

Through a bridle-gate ahead slant into the gill, noting your continuing path slanting up the opposite flank. Cross the beck on suitable stones and take the thin path up the heathery flank to a wall-stile at the top. *Pause to look back over the gill to panoramic views across the dale to Reeth, Calver Hill, Arkengarthdale and Fremington Edge.* A thin path slants up to the right, fading in this pasture but pointing to a gate in a wall rising ahead. Here you meet a grassy track, passing through the gate and rising grandly across part heathery moor to a gate in a wall onto the moor road to Leyburn. Cross onto a green way rising away, then levelling out to run beneath the limestone knoll of Sharrow Hill. Just past an impressive triple-arched limekiln the track fades: a thinner way bears right to contour along to the unmistakeable line of a flue. *This 330-metre long ground-level flue was built to carry fumes from the smelt mill below to a moortop chimney.* Follow its partially collapsed upper section briefly left up to its abrupt terminus at the chimney site.

Here a thin path commences to the right, a fine, level green way through the heather parallel with Cogden Gill. This continues for some time, occasionally slightly faint but traceable until you see a rising track to the right. On reaching a distinctive green ditch turn right down it the few yards to join the track. Double back right down this, merging into another track to slant down to the waiting buildings of Grinton Smelt Mill. *Built early in the 19th century, it operated for the greater part of that century until the industry collapsed. It boasts two well-preserved buildings: the peat store and, by the beck, the mill with numerous interesting features and further information on panels affixed within.*

To resume rise back onto the main track downstream towards the road. A grassy left fork just before it takes you down to where it bridges the gill. Cross and advance just 100 yards to a bridleway heading off left. This path slants pleasantly up across the moor, curving in to cross a dry gill before rising out and following it along to the moor road to Redmire. Cross straight over and away along a similar level, broader grassy way through the heather with the prow of Harkerside ahead. It runs on to meet a rising grass track by a line of grouse butts: the one in front is particularly well concealed. A thin path continues on a short way further to meet a shooters' track. Rise left on this, and at a level section before running on to a small area of spoil at the little gill ahead, leave by a clear path

Limekilns, Sharrow Hill

slanting right down to the stream. It doubles back out the other side and runs on across the moor with a fence nearby on the left. Dropping down to a gate in a fence ahead, it then forks: go left, dropping down close by the left-hand fence again to where it meets a path junction at an intake wall corner.

Through a bridle-gate in the fence (left) head away on a good path rising slightly above the wall. The wall drops away but the path contours on, and the wall soon returns. As it drops away again the path fades just short of a shooters' track ascending the moor. Turn right down this to drop with the wall through a fence-gate and down as a fine green way to a gate onto a back road at Bleak House. *Superb examples of strip lynchets (ancient cultivation terraces) fill the fields across the river.* Cross to a gate left of the house and an old way zigzags down a steep field to a gate in front of a ruinous farm. Now bear right down to a stile part way down, then down to a small gate below, left of a cottage. From another just behind it descend a big pasture to the far left corner, where a stile puts you onto a bridleway by the river flats. Go left to the suspension bridge across the Swale. *This was erected in 2002 after its 80-year old predecessor fell victim to floods.* Across, a path bears right across two pastures to a gate by a barn from where an enclosed leafy way rises to an old lane. Turn right on this - with flags alongside - back into Reeth, becoming surfaced to re-enter the green further along.

Grinton Smelt Mill

3

LOWER SWALEDALE

START Marske   Grid ref. NZ 104004

DISTANCE 6^{1}4 miles (10km)

ORDNANCE SURVEY MAPS
1:50,000
Landranger 92 - Barnard Castle & Richmond
Landranger 99 - Northallerton & Ripon
1:25,000
Explorer OL30 - Yorkshire Dales, North/Central

ACCESS Start from the village centre. Parking area on the west side of the bridge.

> Easy walking links two contrasting villages by fields and lanes

     Marske is a truly delightful place on, but largely outside, the National Park boundary. It differs greatly from other villages of the dale, with its cosy, mellow cottages sat amongst colourful gardens and embowered in noble trees: there is a prosperous country air here of many decades past. The large hall, once home of the Hutton family, survives as flats, and its exterior and grounds still impress. Above the centuries-old bridge is the still older church of St Edmund, with much Norman work. Marske is astride the former main Richmond to Reeth road, and today is known to more travellers as the Coast to Coast Walk passes through.
    Leave the junction along the Richmond/Leyburn road. *Passing the grounds of the hall there is a grand view of its impressive frontage from the entrance gates.* Keep on Cat Bank as far as a bend, then take a wall-stile on the left. *Here begin some grand views over the lower dale, which remains impressively steep-sided and gloriously wooded.* Slant across to an early gap in the hedge by

a water trough, and continue past an island clump of trees to a stile by the bottom corner. Turning up-dale you quickly drop again to a gate to follow the tree-lined Swale upstream to Downholme Bridge, which doesn't appear until virtually upon it. *This is an interesting structure, three arches on an unbroken slant down from the main road: tall limestone scars hover above the wooded bank behind.* A stile admits to the side road.

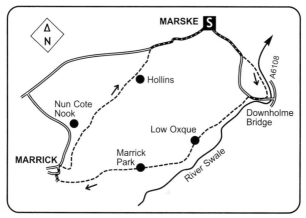

Turn right as far as a bend and then head left along a surfaced farm drive. For some time still in the lovely company of the river, this leads unerringly on (all the way to Marrick, in fact). At Low Oxque Farm it passes along the front and then rises steadily along fieldsides. *As height is gained, improved views over the valley are earned to the moors opposite. A sudden emergence into colourful, open limestone country is heralded by flower meadows in season and an old quarry above your route.* The surfaced drive ends at a collection of renovated buildings at Marrick Park.

Advance straight on between the buildings, and a continuing track resumes the climb. *A restored double limekiln is passed: crumbling limestone walls hereabouts create an impromptu early summer rock garden.* The track runs along a shelf high above the house at Old Vicarage Farm, absorbing its drive. When it swings sharply up to the right it offers a direct route to the edge of Marrick. Better, however, to enjoy a field-path by advancing

19

straight on the wallside to a corner stile. Cross one field bottom to the next then contour across to another. Now cross two small field tops to a gate/stile onto the farm track of Ellerholme Lane. This runs on to meet a back road, where turn right to rise into Marrick.

Go right at the T-junction and right again at the next one, on the 'main street' past the phone box and village hall. *Marrick stands at a blustery thousand feet up, high above the priory of the same name down by the Swale's bank. Founded in the early part of the 12th century for Benedictine nuns, it is visited on WALK 5. Today just a sleepy backwater, Marrick knew far busier times in the hey-day of lead mining. Just off-route to the left are a former church and a former Wesleyan chapel. The observant, on perambulating the village, will discover a number of sundials.*

At the end, as the road swings left out of the village, take the 'no through road' right. This passes the old school before losing its surface at the house behind. *The continuing track is the direct route from Old Vicarage Farm.* Here turn left up a grassy way behind the house (Park Lodge), waymarked for the Coast to Coast Walk. *The return to Marske shares this route, and as such is generally clear. If approaching direct from Old Vicarage Farm, turn right before the first house, Park Lodge, at the start of the surfaced road.*

Limekilns,   *Opposite:*
Marrick Park   *The Swale at Downholme Bridge*

Ascending this short-lived way don't turn into the field on the right, but rise on a path to a small gate at the top. Cross to a gap-stile then up fieldsides with Marrick village to the left. A couple of small, scruffy enclosures are crossed, and finally away from the environs of Marrick's last house continuing along a fieldside. From the stile there the thin path bears right through further stiles, over a gentle brow then drop to a gate to join a farm track with Nun Cote Nook just to the left. *Refreshments are usually on offer here.* Go right the few strides to the wall-corner, then drop to a gate by a barn. Ahead in the bottom is the cottage at Ellers. Continue down through a couple of wall-stiles to pass along the front of Ellers' garden wall. *This lovely house boasts an idyllic, seemingly inaccessible setting.*

Just behind turn down to a stile and a footbridge on Ellers Beck, then slant up the field towards Hollins Farm. Through a corner gate continue up the next field to a gate onto the farm drive. Go right towards the farm (not quite as per map), but turn left up a short wallside track. Curve round to a gate/stile, then slant up to the wall opposite and over the brow to the far corner. From the stile advance a short way along the wall-side until a gate in it, then cross a farm track and over the brow of the last field. Now angle slowly left towards the wall to find a stile onto the road just opposite a cottage. Turn right, and it's now a simple if substantial descent to finish, encased in foliage all the way back down into the village.

MARSKE VALLEY

START *Marske   Grid ref. NZ 104004*

DISTANCE *6 miles (9^{1}2km)*

ORDNANCE SURVEY MAPS
1:50,000
Landranger 92 - Barnard Castle & Richmond
1:25,000
Explorer OL30 - Yorkshire Dales, North/Central

ACCESS *Start from the village centre. Parking area on the west side of the bridge.*

> *Splendidly varied surroundings in a little-known side valley, featuring high quality woodland and moorland*

For a note on Marske see WALK 3. Climb from the bridge to the junction above the church, and take the left branch. When it turns uphill remain on the level cul-de-sac. *Note the sundial on the building of 1607 alongside.* The last house is the former school: here the road loses its surface as it opens out into a field, with views over the valley and wooded banks to the right. Passing the scattered dwellings at Clints, note the former Methodist chapel. A broad carriageway forges on, a charming walk through the sylvan paradise of Clints Wood. Not far beyond the last dwelling the way starts a sustained rise through the trees to a fork: here bear left on a broad path where the main track continues rising. A gate is soon reached to emerge into open pastures beneath the limestone cliffs of Clints Scar. The superb green way runs on to approach Orgate Farm. Just before it turn down the access road to cross Marske Beck by footbridge or ford: Orgate Force is seen just upstream. *The narrow path up the opposite bank to view it is not a right of way.*

The access road climbs to a junction by a large barn, where turn right on the long farm drive to Telfit, shadowing a wall all the way. This quickly passes through a gate into open country beneath the bracken of Telfit Bank. Just before the farm take a gate on the left and a more inviting track scales the hillside, doubling back to a gate. *From this climb up Telfit Bank there are excellent views of the beautiful and remote Throstle Gill, in the upper valley of Marske Beck.* A greener continuation rises gently by a wallside to Munn End Gate to enter the open country of Skelton Moor.

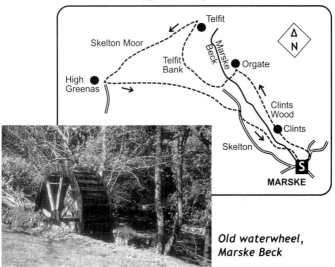

Old waterwheel, Marske Beck

Just ahead is a track crossroads: take the inviting green one straight ahead. *To your right is the remote but colourful country of the valley head featuring the hamlet of Helwith, all beneath rolling moorland.* Rising gently, the track soon eases out amid heather, passing an old sheepfold and a short row of circular bell-pits from lead mining days. Off-route just beyond is an Ordnance Survey column at 1187ft/362m. *The big view from Skelton Moor consists almost entirely of lonely moorland, a notable exception being the mighty keep of Richmond Castle through the portals of lower Swaledale with a long North York Moors skyline beyond.*

The track runs along to a gate into a lane-head. *Here daffodils might be seen pluckily blooming well into June: this is what being 1150ft/350m up in the Pennines brings!* Without joining the lane, remain on the moor by doubling back left on another track which quickly merges with a wall on your right. Now merely a path it traces a long, straight and level course along the wallside, dropping at a bend to arrive back above Telfit Bank. Here you meet the broader track crossed at the start of the moor. *The valley and your outward route appear below.* Bear right on this through a gate in a wall and enjoy a splendid march above the bank on a gently declining, green wallside track. At the next gate it become enclosed to drop down onto a back road.

Turn briefly right to locate a stile on the left after a small barn. Cross the field diagonally to a stile beneath a row of trees, then follow a fence away. When it turns left beyond an intervening bridle-gate go straight on to drop to the substantial stone-arched Pillimire Bridge. *Just before it comes the surprising sight of an old waterwheel now stood in isolation.* Across the bridge a path turns right, crossing the bank to meet the beck again. Here the higher option curves above a potentially muddy beckside section before curving down the bank to a bridle-gate into trees. The beckside path quickly reaches a flight of stone steps up onto Marske Bridge.

Marske church

MARRICK PRIORY

START Reeth   Grid ref. SE 038992

DISTANCE 6 miles (9½km)

ORDNANCE SURVEY MAPS
1:50,000
Landranger 98 - Wensleydale & Upper Wharfedale
Landranger 99 - Northallerton & Ripon
1:25,000
Explorer OL30 - Yorkshire Dales, North/Central

ACCESS Start from the village centre. Roadside parking by the green. Served by bus from Richmond.

Easy walking to an old religious house and its hilltop village, on good paths by riverbank, woodland and through the fields

For a note on Reeth see WALK 6. Leave by the Richmond road at the bottom corner of the green, and along to Reeth Bridge. Soon after it bridges Arkle Beck take a kissing-gate on the right. The path runs between Fremington Mill Farm and the beck. *The building nearest you is the old mill itself, and the drained cut that supplied water from the beck is evident.* Beyond the farm the enclosed path emerges into a field: it short-cuts the beck's confluence with the Swale by veering left, on past a wall-corner to a kissing-gate and then straight ahead to steps up onto Grinton Bridge. *The village of Grinton is immediately over the bridge: see WALK 2.*

Your way crosses the road but not the bridge, and a path enjoys a good spell by the wooded riverbank until emerging into open pasture. Just ahead, a wooded bank forces the path up to a stile onto the Marrick Priory access road. *Easiest option would be to turn right along it to the priory, whose tower is in sight well in advance of reaching it.* A nicer approach is to double back briefly left on the road to a stile on the right. Here begins a largely faint route through the fields, more elevated to give broader views over the valley. Head away, rising gently to find a gate/stile up to the left of a fence corner. *Good views look back up-dale to the Harkerside moors and Calver Hill.* A string of stiles of various design now lead you through the fields, aiming for the priory tower. *A nice wooded bank rises to the left, while Ellerton Moor fills the skyline ahead.* In the last field slant down to a corner gate back onto the road at the farm entrance. *The priory was founded in its pastoral riverside setting early in the 12th century for Benedictine nuns, and the greater part of the remains have been converted into a residential youth activity centre. Access is restricted to a gaze round the exterior. Alongside is Abbey Farm.*

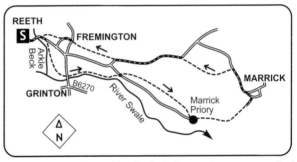

Just after a cattle-grid by the buildings, take a gate on the left where a nice green path rises to a bridle-gate into Steps Wood. A gem of a flagged pathway climbs through it. *Known as the Nuns' Causey, it still serves its original purpose of linking the priory with the village.* On leaving the wood a grassy path remains with the right-hand wall as the going finally eases, and through a gate by a barn it continues as a grassy track to enter Marrick. *As you enter the village the old Wesleyan Chapel of 1878 stands on the left, with the former St Andrew's church of 1858 on your right. The village stands at a blustery thousand feet up, and though today a sleepy backwater, it knew far busier times in the heyday of lead mining. The observant, on perambulating the village, will discover a number of sundials.*

At the first junction turn left up onto the through road, and go left past a farm out of the village. Shortly after a dip beyond a brow, take a stile on the left and follow a wall away. At a stile cross to its other side and remain with it all the way. *An early brow reveals Calver Hill, while Reeth soon appears beneath it, with Swaledale stretching away to the dalehead skyline.* Through two intervening gates/stiles the way runs to a gate onto the old Richmond road at Reels Head. A steep descent of this quiet lane ensues past a well preserved limekiln. *Also well seen during the descent is Grinton, with isolated Grinton Lodge youth hostel high on the moor above.*

Towards the bottom you reach a bend by a drive to West Hag: here a stile on the right sends you off on the last lap. Cross to a stile then on with a sturdy wall until a gate/stile through to the other side. Resume, on through a gate and gateway to cross a field centre to an old enclosed way. Across it a fieldside path runs to a stile onto a snicket on the edge of Fremington. Head along the path onto a narrow lane, following it left and then first right. *This tiny Anglian settlement is divided into two halves: Low Fremington is by the main road, while High Fremington, which you negotiate, is a haphazard grouping of dwellings with an enviable privacy linked by a network of narrow byways.* When the lane quickly swings left to drop steeply down, go straight along a short track to a gate/stile into a field. While the track bears right, a path traces the left-hand wall down to a corner stile, then down again to a stile in your wall. Aiming for Reeth Bridge, cross the field diagonally to a gate/stile with another just beyond it putting you onto the road at the bridge.

Marrick Priory

6

FREMINGTON EDGE

START Reeth   Grid ref. SE 038992

DISTANCE $6^3/4$ miles (11km)

ORDNANCE SURVEY MAPS
1:50,000
Landranger 92 - Barnard Castle & Richmond
Landranger 98 - Wensleydale & Upper Wharfedale
1:25,000
Explorer OL30 - Yorkshire Dales, North/Central

ACCESS Start from the village centre. Roadside parking by the green. Served by bus from Richmond. •OPEN ACCESS, see page 8.

Massive views over Arkengarthdale and the Reeth neighbourhood from a lofty moorland skyline: colourful beckside walking too

Reeth is capital of the whole of Swaledale within the National Park. It boasts an enviable position on the slopes of Calver Hill, well above the Swale and Arkle Beck. It is to the latter of these two watercourses it shows allegiance, with neighbouring Grinton claiming the Swale. Central is a large, sloping green, with the main buildings stood back on all sides. This old market town exudes a confident air, with hoary inns, shops, tearooms and Post office alongside the green: there is also a National Park Centre and craft centre. Reeth caters indiscriminately for dalesfolk and visitors alike, and is the ideal centre for a stay in the valley. Unfortunately parking limitations result in an untidy scene around the green in summer, amplified when market traders set up stall on Fridays. Indelibly linked with the lead mining days, Reeth was once much more populous. There is an absorbing folk museum, while annual agricultural shows and festivals add to its cultural attractions.

Leave by descending the green and following the Richmond road around to Reeth Bridge on Arkle Beck. Immediately after crossing it take a stile on the left and go left along a wallside track. *Fremington Edge dominates high above.* When the track leaves go straight ahead to a gate at the end. Cross to the right of a barn ahead and along to a stile at the end. Now bear right to merge with the right-hand wall, along to a stile in it just above a wooded bank. Leaving the valley floor, cross to a stile opposite then rise on a faint way past a barn to a gate/stile above. Here is a crossroads of ways to which you will return. Now on the steep base of Fremington Edge, take the thin path rising away, bearing slightly left to ascend close by the old wall. This proves a pleasant way as it meanders steeply up, partly-hollowed, enjoying a brief level halt. *Views look back up-dale to Harkerside Moor and beyond Calver Hill.*

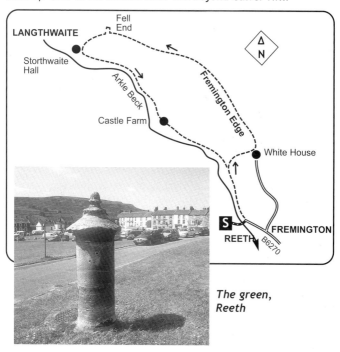

The green, Reeth

Here take the right fork, slanting up a groove then gently up to the top right corner, where a stile deposits you at the isolated White House. A grassy way rises left up the bracken bank to join a stony old road: turn left, passing through a gate. *Scattered around are former chert quarries: chert was a flint used in pottery.* After a little more climbing you gain the crest of Fremington Edge. The track swings sharp right at a guidepost, bound for the watershed wall just ahead: but at this point make use of Open Access as an inviting path runs left through moor grass to enjoy a magnificent stride along the edge. This will remain your course for the march to Fell End. *Relieved of that steep ascent you can fully savour the dramatic views: across the valley is shapely Calver Hill, with tree-lined Arkle Beck far below.*

The path varies in stature but stays largely clear throughout. It rises gently to a substantial cairn amid mining remains, then on to the end of a sturdy wall on the edge. A stile sees you resume, all the way to pass through two crumbled walls. From the second the highest section of the edge at 1510ft/460m is traversed to a redundant ladder-stile at a wall-end. Continue around this high point to a cairn, then a more pronounced drop works its way around the curving edge. *Ahead now are the heathery expanses of Booze Moor beyond the intervening Slei Gill.* Through more old workings the way drops more faintly to a ladder-stile in a wall, then over a broad grassy way and through a minor dip before the slightest of rises to a prominent cairn on Fell End. *Here you are in the midst of much mining remains: be aware that steep, craggy ground drops away beneath the cairn.*

To reach the valley, bear right to pick up a bridleway marked by regular cairns as it passes through the remains of Fell End Mine. Go left on this, dropping grandly between a couple of old ruins. *Booze and North Rake Hush are conspicuous directly ahead across the side valley of Slei Gill.* As gradients steepen bear round to the left, dropping to the foot of a mine-ravaged gully, then swinging right to trace its edge down to a wall. Bear right with it to a gate just short of the corner, where you leave Open Access land. A lush green way descend a fieldside, becoming enclosed at the bottom to emerge at a gate onto a farm lane at Storthwaite Hall.

Go left on the lane to its early demise at a farm, and from a gate ahead a clear path crosses two fields to join Arkle Beck.

Ignoring the footbridge just ahead take the gate in front, after which your path breaks off the bridleway to remain in trees nearer the beck. This it does for some time until reaching a damp, reedy area as the beck swings right. Avoid its excesses by keeping left, through an old wall and along to a gap in another. The stream on your right at this point is merely a rogue branch of the beck. Skirt a moist corner the best you can, after which the way avoids the beck for some while. A faint, partly waymarked path rises gently above the beck, crossing the fields in a largely straight line aiming for the prominent Castle Farm House ahead. Old walls in unkempt pastures are passed through, and a fence on the right also points the way until you rise more pleasantly to a stile in a wall ahead, then on one further small field to the house.

Pass to the left and on through collapsed walls just ahead, then cross to a prominent gap-stile above a steep, scrubby bank. A path then drops away, declining more gently though old walls and past a long-abandoned farm. Just beyond it the beck is rejoined, but on merging with a bridleway at an old gateway just ahead, the broad path forks left, ignoring a path dropping to the beck. After a short amble through trees you emerge through a gateway amid colourful country. The broad path forges on alongside a fading wall on the right. After the second of two further gateways you curve round to the cross-paths on the outward route: through the stile on your right drop down past the barn to return as you came.

Calver Hill from Fremington Edge

MAIDEN CASTLE

START *Reeth   Grid ref. SE 038992*

DISTANCE *5$\frac{1}{4}$ miles (8$\frac{1}{2}$km)*

ORDNANCE SURVEY MAPS
1:50,000
Landranger 98 - Wensleydale & Upper Wharfedale
1:25,000
Explorer OL30 - Yorkshire Dales, North/Central

ACCESS *Start from the village centre. Roadside parking by the green. Served by bus from Richmond.*

A beautiful, richly-varied walk with outstanding views and history

For a note on Reeth see WALK 6. From the green pass along the front of the Kings Arms and the Black Bull to a contrastingly tiny green at Anvil Square. Across it, to the right, a sign 'to the river' sends a snicket off between walls. It emerges onto a narrow road: go left to join a suburban street. Turn left to a T-junction, then right along the narrow lane to its demise at the last house. This continues as a rough lane, with flags alongside. *Across the Swale, Harkerside Moor dominates the dale.* At the end turn left down a narrow, enclosed leafy footway to emerge at a gate by a barn overlooking the river. The path bears right through two fields to reach and cross a suspension footbridge. *This was erected in 2002 after its 80-year old predecessor fell victim to floods two years earlier.*

Although in regular use, the first quarter-mile upstream is not actually a right of way. The true way heads away from the bridge to the foot of the bank ahead, crossing a simple wooden bridge on a drain to turn right with a grassy track past a section of wall. At the wall-end take a bridle-gate in the fence on the right and the grassy path meanders back to the riverbank. Simply forge on upstream in glorious surroundings, largely enclosed by old walls. This delectable section arrives alongside stepping-stones opposite Healaugh. Advance a little further to a bridle-gate, then the path slants left up the steep little bank to join the wall above.

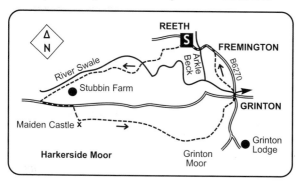

This runs a level course high above the river. *If disappointed at leaving it, think again. The ensuing section is arguably finer still, for in addition to the Swale below, you have outstanding views across to Healaugh backed by Calver Hill, and far up the dale beyond Low Row. The icing on the cake is the lush, green way beneath your feet.* With Stubbin Farm just over the wall, remain with it until passing through a gate/stile in an intervening fence. Here your path bears left up to a gate, just above which a green way rises through some bracken onto the unfenced moor road to Harkerside. *This is the turning point of the walk.*

Double back left up the road as far as the second bridleway branching off right, just as the wall below returns. Don't follow it, but trace the initially less obvious path rising slightly left up the moor. This quickly establishes itself as a fine green path climbing to a lone tree on the skyline just above. Arrival here is a splendid moment, for the hitherto unseen Maiden Castle is literally beneath your feet. *This ancient earthwork is a defensive site of the Iron Age Brigante tribe. A deep ditch surrounds a tall bank, and the whole is largely unbroken other than at the far side, where its gateway is found. Two lines of crumbling walls run directly away.*

The views of Calver Hill and Healaugh remain superb throughout (with notable strip lynchets in the fields up-dale of Reeth), while the dark wall of Harkerside Moor rises directly above.

The path largely fades here: cross to the far side, then simply continue on across virgin heather. This rougher section is quite short-lived, sheeptrods easing progress as you cross to a barn at a wall corner. Here a path slants up to the right, soon forking. Take the fading upper one to rise through heather to quickly meet a very distinct path along the edge of a modest plateau. *High above, still, is the stony scarp of Harkerside Moor.* Turn left on this for a grand stride as it angles very gently down the moor, over an early cross-paths then broadening and passing through a line of grouse butts. Broader still, it drops across to a corner gate where fence below meets wall ahead. *There is a good view of Reeth above the winding river, backed by the unbroken skyline of Fremington Edge.*

Just short of the wall bear right on a thin way joining the clear track ascending from the gate. This rises straight up the moor, but leave it just above the wall corner by trending left across grass to find a clear path forming. This runs a grand course through heather, parallel with the intake wall. *Below is a glimpse of Grinton's church tower.* When the wall comes back to join you it leads the path along to a fence. *Directly ahead across the moor is Grinton's youth hostel, a castellated former shooting lodge.* From the gate a grassy way forges on, ignoring an early lesser branch left. Before long, in fading heather, a distinct green cross-paths is reached. Turn left here, dropping pleasantly down to a gate/stile in a fence by the

wall corner. Following the wall down, a track quickly forms. This slants right to emerge onto the road climbing out of Grinton at the first of its cottages: nicer, however, is to continue down to a small gate alongside a barn below. Continue straight down the field to a stile at the bottom, then down a fieldside until reaching a stile in the wall. A few yards beyond, a slab bridge avoids a marshy drain, then cross to the far corner where a gate sees you out onto a road in Grinton. Turn left down to the junction between St Andrew's church and the Bridge Inn. *For a note on Grinton see WALK 2.*

Cross the bridge and descend steps on the left. The path short-cuts the confluence of Arkle Beck and the Swale by crossing a couple of fields (kissing-gate midway), swinging right alongside a wall in the second one to approach Fremington Mill Farm. At a small gate it becomes enclosed to pass left of the buildings. *Nearest is the old mill itself, with the dry cut alongside your path just past it.* With the Arkle Beck for company the path emerges onto the road at a kissing-gate. With a footway turn left to cross Reeth Bridge, and the road climbs back onto the green. A nicer finish sees you turn down a path on the left signed 'beckside walk'. This doubles back under an arch of the bridge and heads upstream as a darkly enclosed snicket. Keep on to emerge into a pleasant open corner. Go left here up a lane back onto a corner of the main green.

Opposite:
Bridge Inn, Grinton

Maiden Castle,
looking to Calver Hill

CALVER HILL

START *Reeth   Grid ref. SE 038992*

DISTANCE *6 miles (9¹2km)*

ORDNANCE SURVEY MAPS
1:50,000
Landranger 92 - Barnard Castle & Richmond
Landranger 98 - Wensleydale & Upper Wharfedale
1:25,000
Explorer OL30 - Yorkshire Dales, North/Central

ACCESS *Start from the village centre. Roadside parking by the green. Served by bus from Richmond. •OPEN ACCESS, see page 8.*

A memorable ascent of Swaledale's best known and shapeliest hill, featuring delightful heather moorland

For a note on Reeth, see WALK 6. From the green pass along the front of the Kings Arms and the Black Bull to a contrastingly tiny green at Anvil Square. Across it, to the right, a sign 'to the river' sends a snicket off between walls. It emerges onto a narrow road: go left to join a suburban street. Go left to an early T-junction, then right along the narrow lane to its demise at the last house. This continues as a rough lane, with flags alongside. *Looking over the river, Harkerside Moor dominates the dale.* At the end turn left down a narrow, enclosed leafy footway to emerge at a gate by a barn overlooking the river. The path bears right through two fields to reach a suspension footbridge. *This was erected in 2002 after its 80-year old predecessor fell victim to floods two years earlier.*

Don't cross but turn upstream, a good path clinging tightly to the bank until emerging into an open pasture. A delectable section follows on grassy banks. Becoming part-enclosed again the path runs on to a pair of adjacent stiles alongside stepping-stones on the Swale. Leave the river here by following the wallside away to the right, rising to a gate and up onto the valley road at an open green at the entrance to Healaugh. Turn left into the village centre.

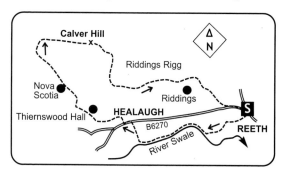

Healaugh was once the important manor herebouts, but today is a sleepy backwater of tidy stone cottages left alone by passing tourists. The Manor House dates from the 17th century. Turn up the side road past a trio of stone troughs, and at an open green at the top bear left on a short access road. Keep left as it runs on by a bungalow, immediately after which turn right on an enclosed grassy path. At the end a corner stile puts you into a field. Cross the field top to another at the end, then bear right through one and away with the wall on your left to a stile onto an enclosed drive. Turn right up this to approach Thiernswood Hall.

The track keeps left of the house to enter trees, becoming a path: at the end ignore the stile in front and take a gate on the right into lovely open country. Rise to find a good stile in the wall corner just above, from where a delightful green carpet rises through bracken. It spirals up in company with the left-hand wall, rising into more open moorland surrounds to meet a rough access road at the lone house of Nova Scotia. Advance on the continuing improved grassy track beyond the house, soon rising grandly through heather beneath a walled enclosure to merge with another track just beyond: wooded Barney Beck is below. Just yards to the left bear right up a thinner, broad way to the corner of another walled enclosure.

This is the walk's turning point. Taking advantage of Open Access, a thin trod ascends past reeds outside the enclosure. At the top corner a grassy way points up the slope above, rising through sparse heather to quickly gain a low nick on the skyline above. *The expansive moorland views are joined by the sudden appearance of Arkengarthdale ahead.* Follow a pleasant path right, raking up the flank to pass beneath a cairn and a rash of stones, with Calver Hill's highest reaches just ahead. Remain on the path which runs a delightful course across a level plateau where the heather peters out. Remain on this path which traverses beneath the higher ground left, on through a further heather patch before slanting left up to a small cairn on the skyline. The substantial summit cairn is just a couple of minutes further.

The summit of Calver Hill is a classic Swaledale viewpoint, with much of the valley on show. More distant features are the A66 crossing bleak Stainmore, and the North York Moors skyline. Leave by dropping away to the right, your goal being a solitary section of sturdy wall on Riddings Rigg, at the foot of the immediate steeper slopes. A faint path slants right down by a scatterings of stones, improving as it curves down to follow the wall down to its far end. Here turn right, within yards a clear path forming in the heather. This drops very pleasantly down to meet a hard access track at a wall corner. *Looking back, Calver Hill forms a shapely crest.* Turn left on the wallside track along the moor edge. When the track finally turns in to a gate, a more inviting track continues on, soon rejoined by the wall to cross pleasantly along the moor edge, the heather now gone but the views remaining wide.

Above the farm of Riddings the track drops gently down. *The full length of Fremington Edge is seen ahead.* As it becomes firmer and bends left, keep straight on the more inviting grassy path ahead to a prominent cairn just short of the next wall-corner. *Here take a final look back to the shapely crest of Calver Hill.* Just beyond is a recess and a gate where a hidden green way known as Skelgate waits to deliver you into Reeth. Its enchanting start is soon overtaken by exuberant undergrowth, and whilst a riot of colour it is not ideal in shorts. As the walls are replaced by foliage the way becomes stonier underfoot. Just past a bend at a crossing farm track take a stile by a gate on the right, and slant left down through a gateway and down to a stile in the bottom corner behind Reeth village school. Just below it a bridle-gate puts you into a short snicket onto the valley road alongside the school on the edge of Reeth. Go left on the footway back down into the centre.

Opposite: Summit cairn on Calver Hill, looking to Fremington Edge　　　*Cottages at Healaugh*

SLEI GILL & BOOZE MOOR

START *Langthwaite   Grid ref. NZ 005024*

DISTANCE *5 miles (8km)*

ORDNANCE SURVEY MAPS
1:50,000
Landranger 92 - Barnard Castle & Richmond
1:25,000
Explorer OL30 - Yorkshire Dales, North/Central

ACCESS *Start from the village centre. Car park on the road above.*
•OPEN ACCESS, see page 8.

> *A richly-varied, colourful walk featuring lead mining,*
> *open moorland and intimate views over Arkengarthdale*

For a note on Langthwaite see WALK 10. Cross the bridge into the heart of the village and turn right behind the first house. A broad track accompanies Arkle Beck downstream before striking away from it into a wood. At a fork keep left, rising out of the trees at a gate to cross a field to another gate. *Views open out to reveal Fell End ahead with Fremington Edge stretching beyond.* While the main track drops right to Storthwaite Hall, your way is the grassy path continuing straight ahead. Ignoring an early fork left for Booze it crosses several enclosures alongside Slei Gill until a stile heralds arrival at the old lead workings. An embanked green track winds straight on between spoilheaps to become a mercurial grassy way. *Slei Gill was the scene of much activity in lead mining days: it is now a peaceful place without the harsher tones of many mining sites. Looking back, Calver Hill rises across the main valley.*

Now becoming more confined by the beck with heather flanks opposite, a superb section rises past modest waterfalls to a small gate onto the open moor, and the path runs along to a large stone arch amid more mining spoil. Here two moorland streams merge: cross the left branch in front of the arch, then rise to a colourful grassy knoll just above. Taking advantage of Open Access, bear left to pass between the left stream and a reedy plateau: a path crosses the marshy outflow and immediately becomes a splendid green way rising through bracken into heather. Keeping right at an early fork it rises delightfully, with the beck guarded by shooting butts over to the left. Further, it leaves the beck to rise more directly, amid less heather, to a wooden shooting cabin, concluding through further heather to meet a level, hard shooters' track alongside.

Turn left along this, quickly reaching a fork at further workings and with a water channel on the left. Although you could remain on either the main track swinging right or the lesser one straight ahead, nicer to eschew the hard surface and trace a bridleway which heads off faintly left. It runs a contouring course parallel with the channel below, swinging right, at times faintly though it maintains a grassy course through heather. It curves right over a very minor brow, which at some 1525ft/465m is the walk's high point.

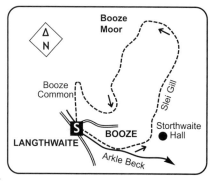

More of Arkengarthdale is revealed as you drop to a mining site. Passing between the first spoilheaps it crosses the earlier drain, with a pool on your right just a little lower. Continue straight down a fading grassy way that ends abruptly in heather. Just to your left a similar way forges on as a thin path down through heather that can be traced down to the earlier hard track above a wall. Your angle of approach may require you dropping right to a gate/stile in the recess, with a barn behind. Having left the moor drop left to a grassy track down the field. When it swings left to a gate continue through dry reeds to a gate at the bottom: steeper ground now drops away. *Lower down but off-route is the hamlet of Booze.*

Advance a few strides to the wall corner on your right, then join a thin trod that clings tightly by the wall as it heads away to Booze Common. It curves round high above the main valley. *This gorgeous, colourful terrain soon reveals Langthwaite below.* On through modest mining remains, a gateway in an old corner wall admits to more open country. The thin trod slants slightly right to a wall-gap then contours round to a fine gap-stile, then on to a crumbling wall corner at the end. *At this point you look directly down on the church.*

The trod resumes with a fence on your left to a stile at the end. A faint way contours above the steep wooded bank demanding a little caution, maintaining a generally level course below a craggy wall (there are also some unseen crags below) and past scattered rocks. At the end is another stile into a field. While the fence drops steeply away, slant more gently down to a corner, then drop left onto a thin bridle-path. Double back left on this through a bridle-gate into the trees, and a super path runs a gentle slant down the wood, featuring a brief walled section before reaching the bottom. It continues for some time before joining the steep Booze road just a minute above the roofs of Langthwaite.

Arkengarthdale from Booze Common

10

ARKENGARTHDALE

START Langthwaite   Grid ref. NZ 005024

DISTANCE 5 miles (8km)

ORDNANCE SURVEY MAPS
1:50,000
Landranger 92 - Barnard Castle & Richmond
1:25,000
Explorer OL30 - Yorkshire Dales, North/Central

ACCESS Start from the village centre. Car park on the road above.

An easy and absorbing exploration of an unfrequented dale

Arkengarthdale is the Swale's major side-valley, and the Arkle Beck is a fast-flowing, tree-lined tributary in keeping with its big brother. Rising on bleak moors near Tan Hill Inn, it takes its name from Arkle Town, a tiny settlement just south of Langthwaite.

Langthwaite is known as the capital of Arkengarthdale, but admittedly its rivals are few. This tiny village comprises of two distinct sections. Along the road through the dale are strewn a miscellany of buildings including the parish church of St Mary, built in 1819 to serve the whole valley. The other half stands just below the road, a cluster of houses grouped on the east bank of the beck. This attractive scene will be recognisable to devotees of the televised veterinary adventures of James Herriot. In amongst these buildings is the Red Lion, one of Arkengarthdale's two hostelries, a cosy little place which has the appearance of a book-shop as much as an alehouse. The other pub is the CB Inn (named after one-time local landowner Charles Bathurst) which stands on the road between the church and the Stang road. Langthwaite was also the centre of the dale's lead mining industry.

Cross the bridge into the village centre, and go left on a short rough lane before the road climbs steeply away. From a gate at the end a path crosses the field, through a gateway to a stile at the end. *En route the village quoits pitch hides over the wall, while above you are lovely wooded slopes.* The way continues on across two more fields to a house in front of Scar House. *This imposing mansion serves as a shooting lodge.* Follow the drive down to join Scar House's wider drive, and head up it a few strides to locate a path through the trees. Over a small footbridge it emerges into a field. The thin path drops down nearer Arkle Beck, past a tiny barn to a stile into a large beckside pasture. This is crossed parallel with the beck to a stile onto the Stang road at Stang Bridge.

Cross straight over to begin an appreciable pull up the back road opposite: this quiet byway is followed for a considerable time. *Early on you rise past former Eskeleth chapel.* Opening out into grassy pasture, it runs on to a gate at High Eskeleth to level out on the

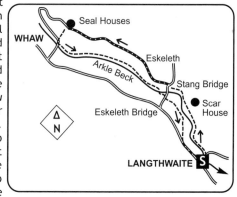

bracken-clad Low Moor. *Looking back, Scar House is seen beneath Booze Common, with Calver Hill also well displayed. The road is sufficiently elevated to give good views across the remote upper dale to the old workings of Whaw Moor and Great Punchard Gill.* Passing through a gate the road leaves the moor. *On the right is an immense limekiln in excellent condition, a useful shelter.*

Continue along the part-open road past a couple more farms at Seal Houses, and leave by a wall-stile on the left. This comes soon after a left fork near a group of modern barns after a farm, and just before another farm. Trending slightly left a direct descent through stiles linking four fields finds a super little path winding down a wooded bank to the hidden hamlet of Whaw. Slanting out of the trees to approach a former chapel, double back left to a ladder-stile to pass the front of a terrace by Chapel Farm onto the road. *The old Wesleyan Chapel dates from 1840, while by the postbox is a former reading room: a small green sits alongside the bridge.* Turn left to the bridge on Arkle Beck. Without crossing advance to a gate downstream, and a faint grassy track crosses three fields to approach the beck. *To the left is an area of old walls and workings.*

A generally thin path continues fairly close by the beck, with particularly attractive wooded moments. Ignoring a footbridge on the beck continue through open pasture, still enjoying the tree-lined beck to emerge by a house. Just beyond, a wooden footbridge is reached just one field short of the graceful arch of Eskeleth Bridge. Cross this and turn downstream to a stile onto the road. Before taking the right-hand of two gates opposite, a short detour up the road is recommended: just over the wall on the right stands a surviving hexagonal powder house from lead mining days.

Back at the gate a drive heads away past a house, with the church in view ahead and Scar House up to the left. Becoming enclosed it swings left towards Old School House: just before it take a stile on the right and a path crosses to join the surfaced Scar House drive just ahead. Follow this right to emerge onto the road at the church. A left turn sees a footway return you through the rest of Langthwaite. *En route you pass a Wesleyan Chapel of 1882, WCs, and a former Wesleyan Sunday School and Institute of 1923.*

The old powder house above Eskeleth Bridge

OLD GANG SMELT MILL

START *Surrender Bridge   Grid ref. SD 988998*

DISTANCE *5³4 miles (9km)*

ORDNANCE SURVEY MAPS
1:50,000
Landranger 92 - Barnard Castle & Richmond
Landranger 98 - Wensleydale & Upper Wharfedale (just)
1:25,000
Explorer OL30 - Yorkshire Dales, North/Central

ACCESS *Surrender Bridge stands at the junction of two moorland roads, a mile north of Low Row, 2¹2 miles south of Langthwaite, and two miles west of Healaugh. It is named on the Explorer map but not on the Landranger map. Parking area at the junction.*

> *Very easy walking entirely on moorland tracks,*
> *visiting outstanding remains of the lead mining industry*

From the parking area descend to cross Surrender Bridge. *Immediately downstream are the remains of the Surrender Smelt Mill, worth a look at the end of the walk.* From the bridge take the road climbing steeply east towards Langthwaite in Arkengarthdale. *Up to your left is a prominent chimney from the Surrender Mill, while to the right is the rangy crest of Calver Hill.* Just before the climb subsides a broad track heads off left to climb unerringly and uneventfully up the moor. *Booze Moor and Fremington Edge are spread over to the right beyond unseen Arkengarthdale.* Ascending into heather, most of the climbing is now done. On levelling out Great Pinseat appears unspectacularly ahead, with a large sheep-fold in front. The track passes through Wetshaw Bottom before reaching the fold. Passing to its left, keep left as a branch goes right beyond it. The track rises left to a big area of mining spoil.

A short way across to the right is a wall running along the top of Great Pinseat: the Ordnance Survey column at 1912ft/583m hides immediately behind it. The track runs on to its own summit at around 1870ft/570m at the next area of spoil crowned by a prominent cairn. *High Dales summits on parade include Whernside, Great Coum, Lovely Seat, Great Shunner Fell and nearby Rogan's Seat, while Great Whernside, Buckden Pike and Ingleborough are well seen across long horizons to the south: lonely Mickle Fell in the North Pennines appears through a gap to the north.*

The track winds through this sprawling spoil a little left of the cairn, then descends through further mining debris to a gate in a sturdy wall. The track now accompanies Flincher Gill downstream, crossing it twice in the process. *In between the crossings you pass by a restored double-arched entrance to a pair of sloping tunnels: well-constructed but unsafe to venture into, they front an old mine level that burrows deep into the hillside.*

**The chimney,
Old Gang Smelt Mill**

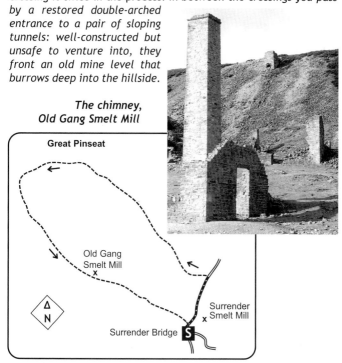

The track continues gently down to reach (but not cross) stone-arched Level House Bridge, where you merge with another track. As Hard Level Gill it leads your track down past much more recent small-scale barytes extraction workings and Hard Level Force in a colourful ravine to the Old Gang Smelt Mill, seen well in advance. Before reaching it you encounter an arched level by the track and a stone-arched bridge on the beck. *Old Gang is one of the best known and most evocative of Swaledale's outdoor mining museums. Having undergone sensitive preservation the buildings are dominated by a tall, intact chimney. On the hillside above are the remains of the former peat store. The mines which the mill served are on the moor west of Level House Bridge.* Remain on the track (the beck is now known as Old Gang Beck) for a further mile back to Surrender Bridge. *Surrender Smelt Mill and Calver Hill*

AROUND LOW ROW

START Low Row   Grid ref. SD 987984

DISTANCE 5$\frac{1}{2}$ miles (9km)

ORDNANCE SURVEY MAPS
1:50,000
Landranger 98 - Wensleydale & Upper Wharfedale
1:25,000
Explorer OL30 - Yorkshire Dales, North/Central

ACCESS Start from the village centre by the church and pub. Roadside parking, with a large lay-by (on route) at the western end just before Isles Bridge. Served by bus from Richmond.

> The attractive surroundings of Low Row feature a superb combination of riverside and moorland rambling

On a shelf high above the river, Low Row straddles the main road for a good mile, incorporating the twin hamlet of Feetham, a name now seldom applied. A long open 'green' runs parallel with the road. The Punch Bowl Inn is an imposing structure dating from 1638, with the modest parish church of the Holy Trinity covering the parish of Melbecks. A quoits pitch sits on the green below the pub, while a nearby cottage bears a lintel of 1693. Hazel Brow Farm is a family visitor attraction which incorporates a café. Further to the west is a United Reformed Church, previously a Congregational Church of 1874.

From the pub head west on the grassy roadside bank past the church to a minor junction. Just beyond this you join the road briefly just as far as the Wesleyan church of 1901. *Alongside is the Literary Institute and Assembly Room of 1909. Behind is a large, sloping burial ground, and a house serving as part-time Post office.*

Here access roads and grass ways on the right keep you off tarmac, running parallel above it past several dwellings. At the last house its access road slants away, but as it doubles sharply back down to the road, go straight on another firm track above a wooded bank. After a ford/footbridge it emerges to start climbing away. Follow it only briefly to by-pass a patch of scrub, then bear left across the sloping pasture. Above a moist spring advance to briefly join the wall below. Before the end a path slants left into trees, dropping to a gate back onto the road. Short-cut the adjacent Crackpot junction by crossing the grassy triangle down onto the side road dropping past Isles Cottages to Isles Bridge.

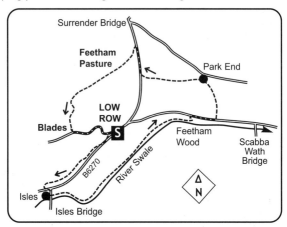

Don't cross but take a path on the left to follow the Swale downstream, clinging to its bank for a good mile and a half. *This section of riverbank, even by Swaledale standards, is sheer pleasure. Virtually the entire length is lined with attractive trees: Low Row scatters most of the way up above.* An intriguing early section runs along the flat top of a wall after which a wooded bend sees more normal progress begin. A flood embankment persists for some time, and further on the path enters the start of Feetham Wood. Soon a guidepost indicates the end of the riverbank stage. Though a thin path continues, the true path is sent left through a moist corner then more comfortably left up the wooded bank onto the road.

Turn right for a few minutes to a solitary house. Immediately after take a stile on the left, and ignoring the Healaugh path sign, ascend past the house to a gateway behind. Now climb the very steep field to a gate at the top right corner. *A welcome pause looks back over the valley, with the long wall of Harkerside Moor beyond a good stretch of river.* Ahead is a surprisingly populated upland scene: cross to a stile then on to the house at Park End ahead, using a stile to its left. Ascend near the wall to a stile half way up, and cross the base of a field to another with a gate/stile behind. Just above is a stile alongside a cottage at Brockma Gill. Noting its steep drive climbing away, you simply take a gap-stile on the left and cross a field bottom to a gate at the end above the next house. Go right to merge into its drive, which leads out past Home Farm as a rough access road to a gate onto a corner of grassy moorland.

Remain on this, passing another house and rising to a brow. Before reaching a farm at Gallows Top, bear right up a faint grassy track, keeping well left of a walled enclosure to rise onto a moorland road. Turn right up this for a few minutes. *Calver Hill makes a shapely sight across to the right.* Ignore two invisible public footpaths signed left until a third one is reached just yards short of the brow. This one is distinct, and doubles back left as a grassy track across the heather of Feetham Pasture. It runs a pleasant, near-level course for a considerable while. *Big moorland views reach from Calver Hill around to Harkerside Moor and Blea Barf.* A slight rise finally reveals the hamlet of Blades ahead. The track runs to a gate in a sturdy wall then drops down to the scattered houses, emerging at the end onto a surfaced road. Turn left down the road which quickly reveals Low Row at your feet and equally quickly deposits you back there.

Isles Bridge

WHITASIDE MOOR

START Healaugh   Grid ref. SE 006983

DISTANCE 5^{3}4 miles (9km)

ORDNANCE SURVEY MAPS
1:50,000
Landranger 98 - Wensleydale & Upper Wharfedale
1:25,000
Explorer OL30 - Yorkshire Dales, North/Central

ACCESS Start from Scabba Wath Bridge, a short mile west of Healaugh on the B6270. There is a large lay-by immediately west of it. Served by bus from Richmond.

> *Good moorland tracks and unsung fieldpaths offer big views from the less frequented southern flank of Swaledale*

Scabba Wath Bridge is an elegant triple-arched structure on the Swale between Healaugh and Low Row. Cross the bridge and go left, bound for Grinton. *The dark wall of Harkerside Moor looms high above.* The narrow back road soon crosses a cattle-grid onto the foot of the open moor, with abundant gorse, bracken and larch providing a colourful scene. The river is soon left behind as this delightful level stroll begins to rise away. *Massive views open up across the valley to Calver Hill above Healaugh.* Before the top, and just before the wall climbs back up again, take a bridleway doubling back to the right through heather. This fine grassy way slants up the moor to soon meet a firmer track. *Low Row is seen straggling along the dale ahead.* Resume up this splendid track at a gentler gradient, levelling out at an old quarry then steepening to rise by spoilheaps from Harker Lead Mine. Easing out again it rises to a level track, where turn right to quickly reach a wooden shooters' cabin. *Extensive views look beyond Blea Barf to Great Shunner Fell, and an unbroken moorland skyline all the way along the north side of the valley.*

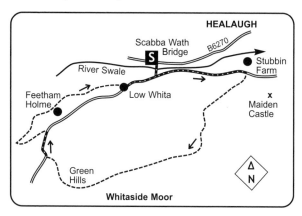

The track crosses deep-cut Browna Gill and resumes across the moor, maintaining a near-level course for some time. When it makes a swing up to the left take an inviting green way straight ahead: this quickly arrives at a magnificent limekiln. Climb the slope after it to rejoin the track and resume. Very shortly a prominent cairn is seen 75 yards over to the right at Green Hills. Cross to this which stands above a scree scarp at 1505ft/459m. Your objective now is a bridleway which might just be discerned half-left down the moor below. You could remain on the track a little further to its official turn-off, but its grassy start is difficult to locate from above. Drop left off this scree edge, passing scant remains of a limekiln and bearing left through virgin heather. Within minutes you will meet the bridleway dropping down the moor. Turn right on its delightful, part-hollowed grassy course down through heather to quickly reach a square, stone fold. Though the path fades here it resurrects just below for the few strides down to a gate in the sturdy intake wall. Pass through it to leave the moor and drop down this rough, part stony pasture. Towards the end a grassy track is reached, going left the few yards to a gate in a wall. This deposits you onto a surfaced back road, High Lane.

Turn right to descend for a few minutes. *Low Row is scattered across the valley ahead.* At a small open area with a seat, take an unsigned gate on the left from where a cart track heads away. This soon turns to drop more roughly and steeply downhill. Becoming enclosed at a gate, drop a little further past a small wood towards a barn. Leave before it at a stile on the right, and slant right to cross to another. This admits onto the driveway of a renovated house. Cross to another stile ahead and one beyond, then a faint trod runs on near the foot of a longer, part stony pasture. Near the end take an easily missed gap-stile in the wall below. Drop to one in the next wall just below, then go right beneath a ruined farm.

A sustained straight march now ensues. Keep on with a wall to your right, through several gap-stiles to approach Feetham Holme. Don't enter but pass to the left and on to the field end. *A long stretch of river is seen beneath Low Row.* Through a stile advance on the field top to the next stile, and cross to a gateway by a barn. Keep on through two further stiles then on to a gate beneath a holly tree, from where slant down to the farm at Low Whita. *Note the distinctive mound of an Iron Age defensive site at How Hill just beyond the farm.* Through a stile above the farm cross to a gate onto its drive, then pass left of a corrugated barn in front to a stile back onto the road by a cottage. Go left the short way back to Scabba Wath Bridge junction. ***Calver Hill and Healaugh from Whitaside***

START *Gunnerside   Grid ref. SD 951981*

DISTANCE *5³4 miles (9km)*

ORDNANCE SURVEY MAPS
1:50,000
Landranger 98 - Wensleydale & Upper Wharfedale
1:25,000
Explorer OL30 - Yorkshire Dales, North/Central

ACCESS *Start from the village centre. Parking area on the west side of the bridge. Served by bus from Richmond.*

Immensely varied rambling takes you from a stunning old bridge amid lush meadows to high tracks and lead mining remains

For a note on Gunnerside see WALK 16, which also explores the gill more fully. From the bridge, depart along the lane to the right of the main up-dale road: it is identifiable by the tidy little village green at the start of it. The lane soon ends at the school, and a gate to its right leads between modern housing to a stile into a field. A little path now heads across several meadows punctuated by a string of stiles (and one gate) to arrive at a bend of the Swale at Marble Scar. Don't take the stile towards the river but go right up the fence-side to a stile at the top above the wooded bank. From here resume as before, through a longer series of stiles all the way to the wooded environs of Shore Gill. Drop down to cross the footbridge and up the other side to emerge into Ivelet. *As you enter note a 1761 datestone by the estate office. Ivelet is a tiny hamlet, off the beaten track and best known for its bridge. You could short-cut the section featuring the bridge and save a mile by turning immediately up the steep road to Gunnerside Lodge.*

Turn down the road to the river, and just along to the right is Ivelet Bridge. *This beautiful old high-arched structure is without doubt the finest crossing of the Swale.* Your route, however, takes a gate on the right to accompany the Swale upstream. Initially you follow the river until deflected right to a small gate at the end of the second field. Instead of returning to the river slant right, a track forming to rise to a gate in the fence above. Slant left above it to a stile in the wall above near the top left corner. The hamlet of Calvert Houses could be accessed by another stile just to the left, but you simply ascend the fieldside to a small gate at the top corner. Now ascend more steeply left to another small gate by an old barn in front of cottages. This puts you onto the Calvert Houses access road. A few yards above, it joins another minor access road.

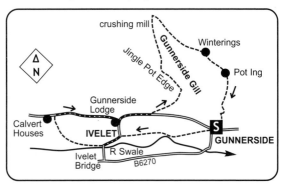

Turn right for a delightful traffic-free stroll. *Grand views are enjoyed from this shelf under the moor edge high above the dale.* Further on it drops down with lush verges to a junction on a brow behind Gunnerside Lodge. Here drop left, the road crossing a bridge and climbing away past Shoregill Head before levelling out along the foot of the open moor. As it starts to drop gently down take a broad shooters' track branching up to the left, in between passing two farms on the right at Dyke Heads. *Ahead are sweeping views over the valley, with Gunnerside itself just ahead.* The track curves left around the hillside to look down on Gunnerside Gill.

Rising along Jingle Pot Edge the track can be seen climbing far ahead, but you leave it before too long by means of a broad grassy way slanting gently right down through reeds. Lower down it improves into a grand old way as it enters bracken and scattered woodland. *Immediately across Gunnerside Beck is a former crushing mill: a long row of bunkers behind was for storing the lead ore.* On the valley floor the path runs upstream to quickly reach a substantial ruin. *This is a former mine shop, an office building of the Sir Francis Mine.* A minute further is an arched level with water emerging beneath a tall wall. Here cross the beck on makeshift stepping-stones to a gate in a section of wall opposite. A grassy path slants right up through bracken to a crossroads with a broader path. Cross straight over and up to approach a sturdy descending wall. Pass right of a low ruin in front of the wall to find an extremely narrow stile in it. Continue across the tops of two fields, emerging into open pasture to advance on a short embanked section. Pass a tiny section of wall (an old sheep shelter) and on towards a wall beyond. Keep well above it to rise gently onto a delectable green track.

This runs on, becoming part enclosed to soon reach the house at Winterings beneath Low Scar. Enter the garden by a gate/stile in front and round to the right of the house. Cross the paddock in front of it to a stile in the wall ahead, into a field. Here begin a splendid crossing of fields linked by wall-stiles: midway there is even a short section of embanked path down into a dip. At the end you approach three buildings, the middle one a barn. Pass right of the left-hand cottage of Pot Ing and on to a gate just beyond, where its grassy drive drops away in sunken fashion. Over a stream and through a gate it rises onto a surfaced road. Turn right to spiral steeply downhill back to Gunnerside far below. *This gentle byway gives a classic bird's-eye view over the roof-tops.*

Ivelet Bridge

15

SWALE'S BANKS

START *Gunnerside   Grid ref. SD 951981*

DISTANCE *4³4 miles (7¹2km)*

ORDNANCE SURVEY MAPS
1:50,000
Landranger 98 - Wensleydale & Upper Wharfedale
1:25,000
Explorer OL30 - Yorkshire Dales, North/Central

ACCESS *Start from the village centre. Parking area on west side of bridge. Served by bus from Richmond.*

> *A simple, intimate riverside stroll*

For a note on Gunnerside see WALK 16. Take the up-dale road out of the village, shadowing Gunnerside Beck to its confluence with the Swale at Gunnerside New Bridge. Across it, leave it rapidly, before the Crackpot junction by a wall-stile on the left. Rise to a small gate just above, then up onto a hard track just above that. This is Dubbing Garth Lane, which now leads unfailingly down-dale to the left. After a stony drop to river level it settles down to a delectable grassy course, largely between walls other than when the Swale is alongside. *Open views look to Rowleth Wood on the north bank and the Harkerside moors down-dale.* Towards the end it becomes a stonier track again to run out through trees to reach Haverdale House Farm. Becoming surfaced it quickly reaches a T-junction with a through road. Turn left and keep left to soon reach the three arches of Isles Bridge (illustrated on page 51). *An attractive row of cottages occupies the far bank.*

Cross the bridge and use a stile on the left to commence the return, immediately abandoning the river to plunge into undergrowth. Emerging, the path bears left along a field and small side-stream, but rather than rejoining the returning Swale it turns away, bearing right by a very low wall. Crossing the trickle, leave the scrubby bank on the right before striking across the centre of a large pasture. Wooden boards at the end cross a linear swamp to a stile behind, then bear right with a wall. Just past a chalet take a gap-stile in the wall and join a grass track running left to meet the valley road as it approaches the returning Swale.

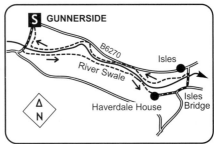

Follow the road briefly left through rich woodland, and as it starts to rise away rejoin the river's bank, a path negotiating scrub before quickly opening out to run a lovely, part-wooded course tight by the Swale. At a stile at the end it is forced back up onto the road at a steep, wooded bank. Head along to another stile, but without setting foot on tarmac take an adjacent gate into a field, and a track drops steeply away. *The village can be seen ahead beyond innumerable parallel walls.*

Whilst the first of a series of stiles in these walls encourages a direct field-path return, it is nicer to bear left to the river. Before the field-end a small gate in the adjacent wall puts you back onto the Swale's bank, and a path follows it pleasurably back to Gunnerside New Bridge. Just before Gunnerside Beck and the bridge, turn for the village at a gate by a barn and cross to a squeezer-stile in the tapering corner. Advance to another into a barnyard, keeping right of the barns to a stile at the end. Through an unkempt corner you emerge into the last field, using a stile at the first buildings (WCs) where the field-path route also comes in to emerge back into the centre, conveniently alongside the pub.

GUNNERSIDE GILL

START *Gunnerside   Grid ref. SD 951981*

DISTANCE *6 miles (9¹2km)*

ORDNANCE SURVEY MAPS
1:50,000
*Landranger 98 - Wensleydale & Upper Wharfedale **and either***
*Landranger 91 - Appleby-in-Westmorland **or***
Landranger 92 - Barnard Castle & Richmond
1:25,000
Explorer OL30 - Yorkshire Dales, North/Central

ACCESS *Start from the village centre. Parking area on the west side of the bridge. Served by bus from Richmond.*

> *A fascinating exploration of a deep side valley with extensive lead mining remains to stir the imagination: a riot of colour*

Gunnerside, like most of its neighbours, had its heyday in lead mining times, when it was a busy centre for the once-thriving industry. Again in common with neighbouring villages, it is now a sleepy place. Founded by Norsemen, it seems Gunnar was a Viking chieftain: until the 1980s the Kings Head sported a superb pictorial sign (see page 8). Village shop and Post office have been lost in recent times, but Gunnerside retains its pub, tearoom, WCs, and a museum at the old smithy. The Literary Institute of 1877 serves as village hall, and there is a Wesleyan Methodist Chapel of 1806.

The village straddles its own beck, which apart from a level quarter-mile from here to the Swale, spends its time tumbling down the deep gill immediately above the village. Gunnerside Gill, even without its open-air mining 'museum', is arguably the most impressive in the Dales. For virtually four miles its steep sides *sweep uninterruptedly down to the beck, with scale and colour of Lakeland proportions. The mines, however, add an extra element, and a gloomy day should be no deterrent to this walk. If anything, lingering cloud adds an almost tangible eeriness to the scene, assisted by the spirits of old miners, perhaps. The lead mines are as much a part of Swaledale as the waterfalls of Keld, and Gunnerside Gill is an excellent venue for their inspection.*

Leave the bridge by an access track on the pub side, following Gunnerside Beck upstream. After having been deflected round Gunnarside Hall, small pastures lead a faint path along more open surrounds until a gap-stile puts you into a wooded bank of the beck. A clearer path now runs by the beck and a few boulders, on through a small gate and into denser woodland. A grand walk leads through this long sliver of woodland from where you rise above the beck. *This early part of the walk, through beautiful woodland contrasts strongly with the bleak scenes which will soon*

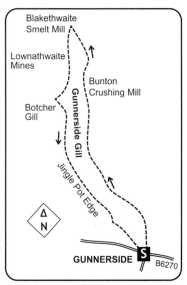

dominate. The wood is left in impressive surrounds as you near Gunnerside Beck again, dropping to a plank bridge out of the trees into an open strath: adjacent stiles send you along a wallside and through two further wall-stiles to reach the site of a crushing mill. *A long row of bunkers just up behind was for storing the lead ore.*

Just past the ruins along this lawn-like flat pasture you reach a fence-stile. Here a path rises to run along a wallside to emerge above a steep bank dropping to the beck opposite a substantial ruin. *This is a former mine shop, an office of the Sir Francis Mine.* Here you leave the valley floor at a stile in the adjacent wall. An inviting, broad green path slants up through bracken, soon levelling out to shadow a wall along, parallel with the beck now far below. As the wall drops away the path rises again, absorbing another path at a cairn. As your path curves up beneath a scar you suddenly find a dramatic scene of devastation greeting the eyes as the extensive lead workings at Bunton are revealed ahead. *This is the site of another crushing mill, with another row of bunkers and many more features in evidence including a prominent level and hushes. In this section of the walk some classic hushes face each other across the gill. These were created by the release of previously dammed-up water which tore away the hillside in the search for new veins.*

Just beyond the last ruin in the immediate workings the path arrives at a staggered crossroads marked by a guidepost on a small knoll: the left fork slants down to the beck and follows it up the gill floor to Blakethwaite Smelt Mill, terminus of the walk. *The smelt mill serving the mines was built around 1820, and its best surviving feature is the peat store, whose ruinous form might be equally at home at Fountains Abbey. A semi-circular kiln sits high on the bank behind, where the old flue rose up the steep bank.* Amidst the ruins a large slab takes you over the beck. *Further exploration might include a couple of hundred yards' detour on a path up the west bank for a closer look at Blakethwaite Force (which is visible from the bridge). Enthusiasts can continue still further up the gill to reach the Blakethwaite lead mines and dams before returning to the smelt mill.*

Back at the smelt mill the return leg of the walk begins by crossing inflowing Blind Gill, from where a superb green way rises gently above the beck. Avoid any deviations and continue to rise to the day's last mining remains at Lownathwaite Mines, featuring North Hush. *The path here surveys the many features of the walk's earlier mining sites from a splendid, detached platform.* The track levels out before it contours around Botcher Gill. Here you merge with a wide shooters' track, which beyond Botcher Gill Gate starts a gradual descent along Jingle Pot Edge, high above the enclave of Gunnerside Gill. When the track eventually curves round to the right, a substantial cairn sends a thin path left down initially reedy pasture. Lower down the terrain improves and a grassy continuation approaches a fence enclosing the wooded gill to reveal the roofs of Gunnerside below: now descend a little more steeply right to an unfenced road as it crosses a cattle-grid to enter the village, or simply follow the fence down to a small gate in the very corner to drop back down into the village centre just opposite the village hall.

A corner of Gunnerside

Opposite: Gunnerside Gill at Bunton workings

ARN GILL & SWINNER GILL

START *Muker   Grid ref. SD 910978*

DISTANCE *6$\frac{1}{2}$ miles (10$\frac{1}{2}$km)*

ORDNANCE SURVEY MAPS
1:50,000
*Landranger 98 - Wensleydale & Upper Wharfedale **and either***
*Landranger 91 - Appleby-in-Westmorland **or***
Landranger 92 - Barnard Castle & Richmond
1:25,000
Explorer OL30 - Yorkshire Dales, North/Central

ACCESS *Start from the village centre. Car park at the eastern end. Served by bus from Richmond. •OPEN ACCESS, see page 8.*

> *An adventurous walk exploring splendid rugged scenery in the Swale Gorge, with a delectable riverbank return*

For a note on Muker see WALK 18. Leave by a road slanting up behind the Literary Institute at a triangular green. Pass to the right of an 'island' residence and then on past the former Post office to a gate/stile out into a field. Initially a track, by the first gate/stile this becomes a well-defined, stone-flagged path crossing seven fields linked by solid stiles to arrive at the riverbank. Turn right to another stile to follow the Swale downstream the few yards to Ramps Holme Bridge. *This tall footbridge is an excellent viewpoint for the lonely Swale Gorge, as far upstream as the cleft of Swinner Gill.* Across, rise a few steps to a fork then go left up onto a level path. Follow this left and as it quickly drops down to meet a stony track, double sharply back right up this. Soon levelling out, make use of Open Access and take an inviting grassy way slanting back left. This begins a mercurial climb through Ivelet Wood, raking ever gently up the flank to break free of colourful scrub. *Views open out over the Swale Gorge and across to Kisdon.* Ultimately it curves round to approach the small sidestream of Arn Gill, reached via mining spoil: just across is a stone hut. Without crossing take a slim trod climbing right, shadowing the near side of the gill to a stone-arched level where you meet the thin trod of a public footpath.

Now cross the tiny stream to a spoilheap, beyond which a thin trod rises gently away, becoming a little clearer on a distinct shelf above steeper slopes. Arn Gill Scar forms up above, and the trod runs on above steep grassy slopes falling to the Swale. This runs a lovely, level course until entering a more pronounced shelf beneath a larger scar. At the end this becomes a sizeable cliff, while ahead is the apparent impasse of West Arn Gill. At the end make a rough slant right into the normally dry gill, rise a few yards then the path escapes up a mini-scramble to resume as if nothing had happened. The path runs a level course to absorb the right of way path slanting in from above, then on to cross the slight trickle of another gill. This one also features a ravine below.

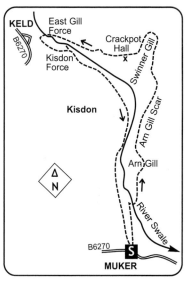

The thin path runs on through bracken and crosses a lesser trickle, then forges on to reach a tumble of large rocks. *The outstanding view now adds Keld to its many charms.* Just beyond the rocks cross to a gate/stile in a sturdy wall. A continuation path slants left above the wall, soon easing and running a gem of a course into the cleft of Swinner Gill. A level stride on a slight bank beneath a low crag leads deep into the confines, with waterfalls and gleaming scars down to the left. Suddenly you find a confluence below you with East Grain climbing to the right, and the remains of

Swinner Gill smelt mill just in front. Curve right to drop to cross the stream to a path on the other bank, and turn left on it between the ruins to curve back round to a stone-arched bridge on Swinner Gill.

The path doubles back out, rising across a small spoilheap, keeping right at an early fork to slant delightfully up across this heather flank. *Look back into the gill to see a fine waterfall beneath the smelt mill.* The path runs on through a few rocks to a gate in a wall. *The Swale makes a fine picture as it heads away downstream.* The grassy way swings right to run through bracken down past an old mine building and beneath more spoil to drop down alongside Crackpot Hall. *This farmhouse was abandoned long ago as a result of mining subsidence: its view down the Swale Gorge remains spectacular.* The continuing track soon merges with one climbing from the left, and swings round to run above a steep, fenced scree slope into the gorge before descending to a stone-arched bridge over East Gill. *Pennine Way and Coast to Coast Walk meet here.* Immediately beneath is the lovely East Gill Force: drop down its far side to appraise it, then just below is a footbridge on the Swale. From it take the path climbing right to a junction where your return to Muker begins: Keld's refreshments are two minutes along to the right. *For a note on Keld see WALK 22.*

The Swale Gorge from West Arn Gill

Back at the junction remain on the upper path which runs on above a wooded bank, opening out beyond a gate a little beneath a limestone scar until reaching a fork. Here stay on the main, lower one dropping through trees. *A short detour to see Kisdon Force takes an early gateway in the wall on the left, and from it a path drops through trees to a viewpoint for the waterfall: the descent to the riverbank is somewhat steep.* Back on the main path it runs an enchanting course to a wall-gate to emerge into the open with the valley outspread and the river just below. A lovely section runs on between low old walls, slanting gently down to lose the walls and on past odd barns. On again, the path meets the valley floor and along a wallside to pass further barns before a stile ahead finally points you to the riverbank. Now simply head downstream for a lovely section on a lush bank. At the end you merge with the end of a wood, and a trickle is crossed to a small gate where you resume downstream just above the river. On through a couple of gates and a couple of stiles, the river has now swung away as you advance to a barn ahead. Pass right of the barn and a grassy way slants up to a gate. On through another one an enclosed section overhung in greenery leads on, opening out again before becoming briefly enclosed to emerge onto Kisdon farm road. Turn down this to re-enter the village just ahead.

In Swinner Gill

IVELET SIDE

START *Muker   Grid ref. SD 910978*

DISTANCE *6 miles (9$\frac{1}{2}$km)*

ORDNANCE SURVEY MAPS
1:50,000
Landranger 98 - Wensleydale & Upper Wharfedale
1:25,000
Explorer OL30 - Yorkshire Dales, North/Central

ACCESS *Start from the village centre. Car park at the eastern end. Served by bus from Richmond. •OPEN ACCESS, see page 8.*

An airy outward excursion with awesome views contrasts with a genteel return from an ancient bridge through riverside meadows

Muker is a good centre for the upper dale, with the Farmers Arms and a shop/tearoom. Muker is probably the most picturesque village in the dale, with a fine grouping of buildings rising above the beck. The River Swale rejoins the main road below the village, after their enforced split by Kisdon. Prominent in most views is St Mary's church, first built in 1580 to relieve Grinton's load, taking off its hands the upper dale: the present structure dates largely from 1890. Other buildings are the Literary Institute of 1868, with the Public Hall of 1922 behind. The old school is now a crafts shop and gallery next to Swaledale Woollens. The village pound stands by the car park entrance. Muker is the venue for the Swaledale Agricultural Show in September.

Leave by a road slanting up behind the Literary Institute at a triangular green. Pass to the right of an 'island' residence and then on past the former Post office to a gate/stile into a field. Initially a track, by the first gate/stile this becomes a well-defined, stone flagged path crossing seven fields linked by solid stiles to arrive at the riverbank. Turn right to another stile to follow the Swale downstream the few yards to Ramps Holme Bridge. *This tall footbridge is the only crossing of the Swale between Keld and Ivelet Bridge, and makes an excellent viewpoint for the lonely Swale Gorge.*

Across, rise a few steps to a fork then go left up onto a level path. Follow this left and as it quickly drops down to meet a stony track, double sharply back right up this. Soon levelling out, make use of Open Access and take an inviting grassy way slanting back left. This begins a mercurial climb through Ivelet Wood, raking ever gently up the flank to break free of colourful scrub. *Views open out over the Swale Gorge and across to Kisdon.* Ultimately it curves round to approach the small sidestream of Arn Gill, reached via mining spoil: across it is a stone hut. Without crossing to it take a trod right, shadowing the near side of the gill up to a stone-arched mine level: here you meet the thin trod of a public footpath.

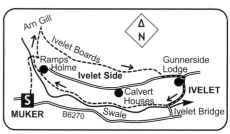

Double back right on this, rising very gently to open out high above the dale floor. It slowly levels out as the modest escarpment of Ivelet Boards forms above. *Be aware that a moderately 'hairy' section awaits, and if wintry or slippery conditions prevail, an option would be to rise to easier ground above the scar.* Advance on to approach a few scattered trees and through small tracts of scree, then easing out on Ivelet Side above further minor scars. *Great Shunner Fell forms a bulky skyline high beyond the huddle of Muker.* A low vestige of wall survives alongside, and as this drops away (directly above Ramps Holme Farm) you now bear off left from the fading edge: a faint but improving way contours round across lovely grass slopes. Passing beneath the more substantial Kisdon Scar and above an old walled lower one (a former quarry), the way reveals the hamlet of Calvert Houses below. The grassy track now drops gently down, passing above an intriguing dark, limestone fissure.

Advance straight on the track's briefly faint course before improving through moor-grass and reeds to quickly join a firm shooters' track. Turn down this above the wooded side gill of Grains Gill onto the open road below, and go left. Lush, grassy verges lead along to a junction behind Gunnerside Lodge, Swaledale's premier shooting lodge. Turn right to descend to the cosy hamlet of Ivelet. Continue down the road from Ivelet to the river, and just along to the right is Ivelet Bridge. *This beautiful old high-arched structure is unquestionably the finest crossing of the Swale (see page 57).* Your route, however, takes a gate on the right to accompany the Swale upstream. The way is straightforward, with an intermittent path staying close to the river after an early detour to pass through a small gate at the end of the second field. *The path alongside the Swale witnesses good scenery as it flows over a wide, stony bed.*

After a long mile the path cuts out a bend in the river by being deflected by a small wooded bank, on through a gateway where a short track drops down, then briefly back with the river as you advance on through a gate/stile back onto the bank. At the end take a gap-stile and forsake the river by crossing several stiles in parallel walls to pass the front of Ramps Holme Farm. From a stile by a barn beyond the farm a path runs on above a wall to rejoin the outward route, dropping down to re-cross Ramps Holme Bridge and retrace steps through the fields back to Muker. *Muker*

19

MUKER SIDE

START Muker   Grid ref. SD 910978

DISTANCE $5^1/4$ miles ($8^1/2$km)

ORDNANCE SURVEY MAPS
1:50,000
Landranger 98 - Wensleydale & Upper Wharfedale
1:25,000
Explorer OL30 - Yorkshire Dales, North/Central

ACCESS Start from the village centre. Car park at the eastern end over the bridge. Served by bus from Richmond.

A simple walk offering stunning views from low slopes and linking two delightful upper dale villages

For a note on Muker see WALK 18. Cross the bridge at the east end of the village and follow the road down-dale for a few minutes. At a bend beyond a small barn leave at a kissing-gate on the right. Follow the wall away towards a barn but then bear left, crossing a stream and onto the top of a wooded bank. Towards the end bear right to a stile with a house behind. Pass along the front and on the wallside to a corner stile. From one in the wall behind slant up a larger pasture to the further of two houses at Rash. From a stile above it a drive is joined by the house: turn right on this to Rash Grange. Pass along the top of the house to a gate from where a grassy track rises away. Don't follow it but take a thin path dropping right a few steps to run on above a wall. *Improving views look across to Muker and further up-dale.* Apart from an early slant up to a corner this same path runs an undulating course always with or just above the wall, through a small gate and on to eventually drop to a gate onto a walled track, the Occupation Road.

Turn left up this for a long slant up towards Muker Side. *An old kiln lurks in undergrowth on the left. Increasingly magnificent views look across the valley to Kisdon, while beyond Muker is the Swale Gorge backed by Rogan's Seat.* Ultimately the way swings left to rise to a T-junction of walled tracks at Three Loaning (lane) End. Go right for a near-level stride along Muker Side. *This super section enjoys truly outstanding views over the upper dale, in particular across to Kisdon and the Swale Gorge behind Muker: Great Shunner Fell impresses straight ahead.* Just beyond crossing a stone-arched bridge on a tiny stream, turn right down a walled, grassy way as far as a tiny barn on a bend. Here leave by a gate on the left, crossing a field-bottom to become briefly enclosed again as a green way before a continuing track passes above the renovated Appletree Thwaite. Merging with its drive at a gate at the end, follow it down through a further gate then down a larger field to find a stile just to its right in the bottom corner. This gives a tiny short-cut over a footbridge on Cliff Beck in a lovely little ravine. The track is rejoined just beyond to run out onto the road, with Thwaite just along to the left beyond the Hawes junction.

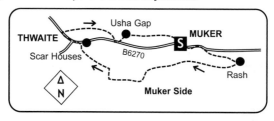

If there is a reasonable amount of water in the lively beck under the footbridge, then a very short detour is recommended. Take a gate on the right just after the bridge and descend the field to a stile onto the road at Scar Houses. Walk just a few yards right to see a charming waterfall on the same beck, just above the road. Retrace steps along the road to drop down into Thwaite. *Thwaite is a tiny village that long remains a happy memory to the Pennine Wayfarers who descend from the long, hard miles of Great Shunner Fell. The place they seek sanctuary recalls another memory, that of local lads Richard and Cherry Kearton, nature photography pioneers. The popular Kearton Country Hotel offers refreshments.*

Turn along the short lane in front of the Kearton teashop, and at the end a Pennine Way sign points through a short enclosed path by a house just right of a farmyard: a couple of stiles lead into a field. Here the Pennine Way strikes left, but you continue with Thwaite Beck to a wall-stile ahead. Here leave the beck for a thin path across three further fields to reach a stone-arched footbridge over a smaller beck, Skeb Skeugh, coming in from the left. Beyond a stile head away with a wall to a stile at the end, then on past a barn to a stile from where a short, enclosed beckside track runs on to join the road at Usha Gap Bridge.

Go left along the road to the farm and up to the house. Go right through the yard to a gate into a camping field, then bear left to a stile near the far end of the field. From here a string of very obvious stiles leads a faint path across a host of field-bottoms to Muker, waiting ahead. *The latter stages of the path are flagged.* Emerging into the village, a little snicket on the right drops rather conveniently down to emerge alongside the pub.

Muker and Kisdon from the
Occupation Road under Muker Side

AROUND KISDON

START *Thwaite   Grid ref. SD 892981*

DISTANCE *5$\frac{1}{2}$ miles (9km)*

ORDNANCE SURVEY MAPS
1:50,000
*Landranger 98 - Wensleydale & Upper Wharfedale **and either***
*Landranger 91 - Appleby-in-Westmorland **or***
Landranger 92 - Barnard Castle & Richmond
1:25,000
Explorer OL30 - Yorkshire Dales, North/Central

ACCESS *Start from the village centre. There is limited roadside parking, but more space on the road dropping into the village from the Buttertubs junction. Served by bus from Richmond.*

A magnificent walk encircling a colourful little fell: classic views

Thwaite is a tiny village that long remains a happy memory to the Pennine Wayfarers who descend from the long, hard miles of Great Shunner Fell. The place they seek sanctuary recalls another memory, that of local lads Richard and Cherry Kearton, pioneers in nature photography. The popular Kearton Country Hotel offers refreshments: turn along the short lane in front of it, and at the end a Pennine Way sign points the way through a short enclosed path by a house just right of a farmyard: a couple of stiles lead into a field where the path forks. Go left on the Pennine Way, across to a gate and on a grassy track to a farm bridge on Skeb Skeugh. Bear right up the steep field, merging with a wall to rise to a corner stile onto open moorland. A super path slants up through heather to a wall corner. *This stage has sweeping views back over the village to Lovely Seat, Buttertubs Pass and Great Shunner Fell.* Head on with the wall around above a barn with a glimpse of Muker, up to a stile and on with a wall on your left. This curves round to become briefly enclosed, on through a small gate then swinging right with the wall to run to the rear of Kisdon Farm.

Passing through a gate at the end onto the drive, instead take a gate on the left from where a green walled way rises past an old limekiln. Quickly opening out at a fork the Pennine Way turns briefly right to the start of an enclosed way, then goes left to rise above a barn. At the wall ahead ignore the continuing green track rising left, and pass through a ladder-stile in front to commence a classic walk along the terrace of North Gang Scar, passing through various gateways and stiles and an occasional rash of stones. *This traverses the flank of Kisdon in glorious fashion, one of the top ten highlights of the Pennine Way. Spectacular views look over the finest section of the Swale backed by Arn Gill and Swinner Gill under Rogan's Seat. Kisdon, which rises to 1637ft/499m, is a fell detached from others at the end of the Ice Age. As a result the Swale was deflected from its original course around the west side of the hill, a route now used by the motor road.*

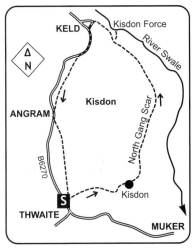

Eventually a wooded bank comes in on the right and the path follows the hillside round to the left for a sustained spell. In time a fork is reached at a gap in the accompanying wall. Pass through to slant down to a junction with a broader path. Keld is but a few minutes along to the left, but for a short detour to see Kisdon Force, go right. Just down a slope is a gateway in the wall on the left, and from it a path goes down through the trees to a viewpoint for the waterfall. The descent to the riverbank is somewhat steep. To return to Keld rejoin the top path and go back along to the right now, passing beneath tall cliffs before the way becomes enclosed to enter the village. *For a note on Keld see WALK 22: refreshments are often available at Park Lodge just across the square.*

From the square climb to the main road and turn left out of the village. A little beyond a bridleway on the left a stile will be found. Drop down a little and cross to a stile ahead. Here begins a field-path marked by regular stiles: in early summer these flower-rich meadows ensure a delectable path. Early on, where you don't see a stile, simply cross to a footbridge on a sidestream to resume. A further guide is a string of field barns all passed on their right. *A brow beneath the hamlet of Angram reveals Thwaite with Lovely Seat above: to your left Kisdon's western flank looks splendid.*

The road is rejoined at a stile after skirting Angram, and within a couple of minutes is vacated again at a gate/stile on the left. Slant down to find a stile beyond an island barn, then on to bridge a stream. Through a stile just beyond follow the left-hand wall away through several pastures. At a stile by a barn the wall ends and you cross to another stile/barn at the end. A moist corner leads on, now alongside tree-lined Skeb Skeugh. A part-flagged path runs to a corner stile, then an embanked path bears left to another corner stile. Continue on through a gate/stile, and left of some barns to a stile onto the start of the walk, turning right to re-enter Thwaite.

On the path along North Gang Scar

KELD WATERFALLS

START Keld   Grid ref. NY 892011

DISTANCE 4³4 miles (7¹2km)

ORDNANCE SURVEY MAPS
1:50,000
Landranger 98 - Wensleydale & Upper Wharfedale **and either**
Landranger 91 - Appleby-in-Westmorland **or**
Landranger 92 - Barnard Castle & Richmond
1:25,000
Explorer OL30 - Yorkshire Dales, North/Central **or**
Explorer OL19 - Howgill Fells/Upper Eden Valley

ACCESS Start from the village centre, down from the main road.
Limited parking, but adjacent Park Lodge operates a car park.
Otherwise, park on the main road. Served by bus from Richmond.

A moorland spell sandwiched between waterfalls and meadows

For a note on Keld see WALK 22. From the square climb to the
main road and turn left along it. A little beyond a bridleway on the
left a stile will be found. Here begins a field-path marked by stiles
at regular intervals: in early summer these flower-rich meadows
ensure a clear, delectable path. A string of stiles is mostly visible in
advance: early on, where you don't see one, simply cross to a footbridge on a sidestream to resume as before. A further guide is a
string of isolated field barns that are all passed on their right. *A
brow beneath the hamlet of Angram reveals Thwaite ahead with
Lovely Seat above: to your left Kisdon's western flank remains a
splendid sight throughout.*

The road is rejoined at a stile a little after skirting Angram.
Turn back up the hill into the hamlet and take a road doubling back

up to the left by the phone box, noting the 'Angram AD 807' stone. Leave virtually at once by a gate on the right, and follow a sunken way up the field above a wall. Just beyond an old limekiln you pass through a gate for a brief enclosed section, then the track heads away, becoming fainter as it slants up the rough pasture to a gate in a rising wall. *Extensive views look over Keld to Rogan's Seat, and back over Angram down the upper dale backed by Lovely Seat.* Follow a wall heading away along the edge of a tract of heather moor, and as it drops away contour along to a stile in the wall ahead.

Head away from this on a thin way, crossing a reedy dip to another stile in the facing wall. Now bear gently left up the next pasture, with a large tract of heather moor across Ay Gill just ahead. A pathway forms at the corner of

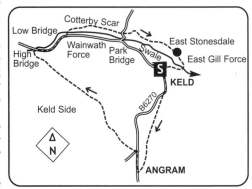

ruinous walls (note the covered watercourse), and this lovely grassy way runs on above the stream and attendant wall. It drops to run along to join the wall, and quickly takes a stile in it to enter the heather moor. A clear path runs left along the edge of the moor to a stile back out at the end. *At around 1410ft/430m this is the summit of the walk on Keld Side. Ahead are vast sweeping views to the high watershed of the Swale, featuring the High Seat ridge and Nine Standards Rigg. Over to the right the limestone cliff of Cotterby Scar is well seen: shortly you shall be walking above that.* A thinner but still clear path now runs very gently down through moor grass to a wall-stile. More scattered heather is entered as the path runs on to drop down to a hard shooters' track, reached by crossing a log bridge on Blackburn Beck lined with grouse butts.

The continuing path is indicated by a small cairn virtually opposite: head away on a broad, grassy section between the

heather. A faint pathway slants left up this, appearing to be heading the wrong way as it rises to the left. It soon forks however, and
a right turn sees a clearer path form in the heather. This runs down
to a ladder-stile off the moor in the wall ahead. Two pastures are
crossed diagonally to reach a third ladder-stile. *Ahead is a lovely
prospect of the Swale below Hoggarths Farm, backed by high fell
country.* A clearer quad track now completes the slant as it angles
down to join a firm track by the river. Double back right on this the
short way to the road at High Bridge.

Turn right along the road, passing a splendid waterfall on the
infant Swale before climbing above the river. *This gives a super
prospect of the confluence of Whitsundale Beck with the Swale.*
Dropping back to the river, cross stone-arched Low Bridge on the
left at the beginnings of Cotterby Scar. As the track climbs away
past a limekiln built into the hillside, leave it on reaching the first
trees, by a gateway in the old wall on the right. A thin path (the
Coast to Coast Walk) doubles back alongside the wall to commence
a level stroll above the full length of the top of Cotterby Scar.
*Though a grand path, it offers only glimpses of the scar itself.
Bluebells take advantage of the shelter of the trees atop the scar.*
From a gate at the end the way shadows an old wall across open
pasture: Wainwath Force below is largely obscured by trees. At a
fork keep straight on along the field top to a gate onto the Tan Hill
road. *The thinner right fork, incidentally, drops to a corner stile
onto the road to join the B6270 for a quicker return to Keld, with
a better view of Wainwath Force just upstream of the bridge.*

From the top gate, cross straight over the road and head away
along the drive to East Stonesdale Farm. *Approaching Stonesdale
Beck you hear the sound of Currack Force, an unsung gem just off
the track before the bridge.* A little pull precedes a level stroll to
the farm. *Keld looks precariously placed on a steep shelf above the
river.* Passing above the farm the Pennine Way is joined. Turn down
through a gate at the end and the track drops steeply to a junction
with the Coast to Coast Walk at East Gill Force: ignore the bridge
ahead and drop down this side of the falls. *With the end now only
minutes away, this delectable spot is worth a few minutes of
anyone's time.* Take the path down the near side of the waterfall
to a footbridge on the Swale. The path climbs up to the right, and
keep right to run enclosed back along to re-enter the square.

22

SWALE GORGE

START Keld   Grid ref. NY 892011

DISTANCE 6 miles (9$\frac{1}{2}$km)

ORDNANCE SURVEY MAPS
1:50,000
Landranger 98 - Wensleydale & Upper Wharfedale **and either**
Landranger 91 - Appleby-in-Westmorland **or**
Landranger 92 - Barnard Castle & Richmond
1:25,000
Explorer OL30 - Yorkshire Dales, North/Central

ACCESS Start from the village centre, down from the main road. Limited parking, but adjacent Park Lodge operates a car park. Otherwise, park on the main road. Served by bus from Richmond.

> A beautiful, easy walk through stunning scenery: do it!

Keld is the first outpost of any size in Swaledale, beyond here are only isolated dwellings beneath the moors. Most of this Norse settlement is set around a tiny square just below the main road. Here is the Public Hall & Reading Room of 1926, with refreshments available at Park Lodge. Just along from it a chapel of 1861 boasts a fine old sundial: alongside are WCs and old Institute, while the Great War memorial remembers four men who never returned to their farming hamlet. The fact that this delectable spot marks the junction of Pennine Way and Coast to Coast Walk was insufficient to save its youth hostel from closure: today the former shooting lodge of Keld Lodge may be a more expensive replacement, but its welcome presence has brought licensed premises back to Keld for the first time since the closure of the Cat Hole Inn in the 1950s. Just along from it is a Methodist Chapel of 1841. Keld is famous for its waterfalls, one seen here and others on WALKS 20 and 21.

Leave the square by the road rising left to the main road, and turn left along it until a walled track drops down to the left by a barn. This old way will lead unerringly over the hill to Muker. *It is the first and most impressive section of the former 'corpse road' which ran all the way down the valley to Grinton. For the deceased of the Keld area it was only the start of a long trip for burial prior to Muker acquiring its own consecrated ground.* Crossing a tiny beck by ford and slab footbridge it begins to climb steeply away, soon opening out until it slants up an open pasture as a fine green way. *There are good views of the mountains around the dalehead, all 2000-footers from Lovely Seat to Great Shunner Fell, High Seat and Nine Standards Rigg. Opposite is the hamlet of Angram.*

Easing out further the track runs on beneath a very isolated house, and when it swings left to serve it an even nicer green way continues on to a gate in a wall ahead. A long pasture is crossed, still rising gently until approaching Hooker Mill Scar just ahead, it swings left up to a gate in the parallel wall. Rising to another such gate it then runs on between old walls by mining debris. Through a further gateway it runs along the edge of moor-land. *The unfrequented summit of Kisdon stands at*

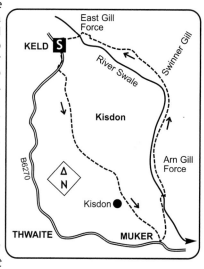

1637ft/499m a good half-mile over to the left. Arrival at a gate in a wall ahead finally marks the summit of the walk at around 1607ft/490m. *By now the first views ahead have appeared, with sombre moors across the gorge leading round to Rogan's Seat.*

The way drops away with a wall on the left. *Quickly revealed are Swinner Gill, Arn Gill and Ivelet scars opposite and more of the main valley.* Muker shortly appears and the way soon short-cuts the true line which drops to the corner then turns right, slanting down to become enclosed at the far corner. *The steep descent to Muker reveals views beyond the village at your feet, and far down the dale.* Emerging, continue down the wallside to meet the Pennine Way coming in from the right. With a wall on your right follow it for just 50 yards, and as it swings left at a barn continue straight down, briefly enclosed again, to emerge at the bottom onto Kisdon farm road. Muker re-appears truly at your feet as this well-surfaced way takes you steeply down through two final pastures to enter the village along a short lane. *For a note on Muker see WALK 18.*

Leave by a road slanting up behind the Literary Institute at a triangular green. Pass to the right of an 'island' residence and then

on past the former Post office to a gate/stile out into a field. The Swale Gorge fills the scene ahead, and how! Initially a track, by the first gate/stile this becomes a very well-defined, stone flagged path which crosses seven fields linked by solid stiles to suddenly arrive at the riverbank. Turn right to another stile to follow the Swale downstream the very short way to Ramps Holme Bridge.

The Swale at Ramps Holme Bridge

This tall footbridge is the only crossing of the Swale between Keld and Ivelet Bridge. It makes an excellent viewpoint for the lonely Swale Gorge, upstream to the cleft of Swinner Gill. On the opposite bank drop down left to the river and soon a wide track is joined. With good verges it is accompanied almost all the way back to Keld. On crossing the first inflowing beck, stroll a short distance up its course for a fine view of the charming waterfall of Arn Gill Force tumbling through foliage. Continuing, the track rises a little above the river to run on to cross a bridge below the ravine of Swinner Gill. *The steep-sided gill above your crossing was once a thriving lead mining scene: it is explored in WALK 17.*

The track then rises steeply before easing out above an increasingly impressive wooded, rocky gorge. A track from the ruin of Crackpot Hall is joined, and this same track runs left on above a steep, fenced scree slope into the gorge before descending to a stone-arched bridge over East Gill. *The Pennine Way and the Coast to Coast Walk meet here.* Immediately beneath is the lovely East Gill Force: drop down the far side of the waterfall to appraise it and then just below is a footbridge over the Swale. From it take the path climbing right to a junction, there going right and within minutes Keld is re-entered.

East Gill Force, Keld

WEST STONESDALE

START Stonesdale   Grid ref. NY 884044

DISTANCE 7^{1}4 miles (11^{1}2km)

ORDNANCE SURVEY MAPS
1:50,000
Landranger 91 - Appleby-in-Westmorland **or**
Landranger 92 - Barnard Castle & Richmond
1:25,000
Explorer OL30 - Yorkshire Dales, North/Central **or**
Explorer OL19 - Howgill Fells/Upper Eden Valley

ACCESS Start from the Keld road 1^{3}4 miles south of the Tan Hill
Inn, where Lad Gill is crossed by a stone-arched bridge at Point
411m on the map, up-dale from Stonesdale Bridge. There is verge
parking just below it. •OPEN ACCESS, see page 8.

> *Surprisingly easy walking over bleak moors*
> *enveloping colourful side valleys*

Leave the road by a rough track on the downstream side of the
bridge, rising near the sidestream of Lad Gill to soon meet the
Pennine Way path that has just crossed it. Turn right on it, looking
down to a nice waterfall on Stonesdale Beck immediately below
the start-point bridge. The path runs on, and beyond a tiny sidestream is a fork: take the main one rising very slightly left, aiming
for the nearest of a collection of barns ahead. *The Tan Hill road
now runs a parallel course across the deepening gill.* Here a firm
track becomes briefly part-enclosed to reach the next barn alongside a spring. The drive to isolated Frith Lodge is met here, and
runs a splendid level course straight ahead. *Below, the valley of
West Stonesdale now takes a better-defined shape.*

Directly beneath the house the track turn up towards it: here keep straight on a grassier way to a gate. *Behind it is a tiny stream resplendent in mixed foliage as it tumbles steeply down.* Here turn down to the right, forsaking the inviting green way that runs ahead. Drop to join the wall just below to quickly reach a stile in it. *Note the attractive little arched bridge on the beck just upstream.* Slant left down the large, colourful pasture to the nearest barn, and from a stile in the wall to its left, cross the field to join West Stonesdale Beck. Ignoring a bridge turn downstream, passing a ford and along a thin trod through a bridle-gate and then a stile to reach a foot-bridge. *This is a grand spot, as the bridge straddles a small ravine with tumbling waters.* Across, a little path runs briefly down-stream, then bear left up the steep field to a gate near the top. Go left along the field top at the rear of cottages to a gate at the end onto the road at West Stonesdale, a tiny farming hamlet.

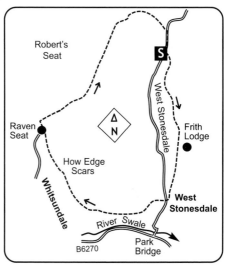

Go left to the phone box, just past which a short-lived way rises by beck and cottage. From a gate ahead climb between the left-hand wall and the gill onto open moor. Remain near the wall as the going eases and the wall bears left. *To the left are good views of Keld, with Kisdon and the Swale Gorge beyond.* The wall remains a close companion for the next mile as useful sheeptrods can largely be traced across the grassy moorland a short distance above it. *Over to the left are the vast, sprawling slopes of Great Shunner Fell, with sections of the Swale upstream ahead.*

When the wall finally drops away to a track, keep straight on around the hillside, still on no more than sheeptrods and gaining a tiny amount of height. The terrain remains good as the parallel Coast to Coast path runs through less endearing reeds just below. The slope leads round to a massive, circular crumbling sheepfold. The likelihood is you will have merged with the lower path just short of the fold, though the better line of the right of way passes above it, a little beyond which a good grassy track slants down to join the Coast to Coast path just yards short of the end of this open pasture. With a gate into the first of a succession of pastures just ahead, this moment is memorable due to you being perched directly above the stunning scenery of Oven Mouth, where craggy and colourful slopes plunge to a splendid ox-bow on Whitsundale Beck.

The path runs on a wallside through two further gates in cross-walls, emerging into rougher pastures to look down on the ravine of How Edge Scars, another super spot. On through a couple of gateways a barn is passed, and at the next barn the path advances to one just yards further, revealing Raven Seat just ahead before slanting pleasantly down to a gate to gain the bank of the beck at a waterfall. Turn upstream through two final pastures to approach Raven Seat. *This tiny farming hamlet is more than a little off the beaten track, an oasis of green fields in a moorland hollow: refreshments are often available at the house across the beck.*

Entering the first enclosure with a cottage on the right, don't turn down to the farm bridge over to the left. *While the original route passes between barns to cross a charming arched footbridge to the farmyard before taking a track up-dale, a permissive path saves you having to ford the beck.* Go straight ahead to a gate/ stile. *Having sampled both Pennine Way and Coast to Coast Walk, you are now almost certain to be alone.* Head upstream past an intact stone sheepfold to a gate in the wall ahead. Here cross a sidestream to join the right of way which has just forded the main beck on a track below. Turn right up this track, through a gate/stile to begin a sustained pull up the side of the pasture in the company of the small, deep gill of Pryclose Gutter, with newly planted trees. Veer slightly left at the top to a fence-stile onto the grassy moor.

A path rises left towards a TV booster on a small quarry site, then bears right beneath it to a crumbling stone hut amid scattered rocks (approaching the hut is a fork, but they rejoin on reaching it).

Slanting up around it, Tan Hill Inn appears on the skyline ahead, not looking too distant with the road climbing to it. *The wild surrounds feature Rogan's Seat ahead, the pudding-like Kisdon, and round to Lovely Seat and Great Shunner Fell.* Just ahead is a fence, and from the stile the path continues on through excellent terrain, with a gentle rise to your left and a peaty plateau below. *With the larks singing and a pub on the horizon, all is wonderful: the slim trod forges on its delightful grassy way with sweeping moorland vistas.*

With Robert's Seat to the left, the way keeps just right of the minor watershed to maintain its contour, the dry terrain eventually giving way to a short mossy spell. Things soon improve again and the path drops very gently right, soon running on more decisively again along the crest of a distinct grassy spur: to your left is a tiny stream. Now doubling as a quad track it leads clearly on, gently declining to an emphatic halt above Thomas Gill, a veritable impasse. The path swings down the near side of this scarred ravine to drop to a crumbling sheepfold complex. Immediately below the confluence with Stonesdale Beck is a neat little stone footbridge. Across, turn downstream a few yards to a ford, and follow the track slanting up through reeds to a bend of the Tan Hill road. Turn right for a very gradual descent back to the start.

Old bridge at Raven Seat

BIRKDALE & WHITSUNDALE

START Hoggarths   Grid ref. NY 870013

DISTANCE $5^1 4$ miles ($8^1 2$km)

ORDNANCE SURVEY MAPS
1:50,000
Landranger 91 - Appleby-in-Westmorland **or**
Landranger 92 - Barnard Castle & Richmond
1:25,000
Explorer OL30 - Yorkshire Dales, North/Central **or**
Explorer OL19 - Howgill Fells/Upper Eden Valley

ACCESS Start from High Bridge, below Hoggarths farm on the B6270 a good mile past the Tan Hill junction west of Keld. Parking area immediately over the bridge. •OPEN ACCESS, see page 8.

> *Two lonely side valleys mark the transition from rough moorland to the first scattered fields of Swaledale*

From the Keld (east) side of the bridge take a track running upstream, and just through a gate fork left between a stream and a wall. At a barn take a gate to its right and continue on a level course, soon leaving a wall behind and joining the riverside. *The Swale is formed by the meeting of Birkdale Beck and Great Sleddale Beck, and consequently your first mile is also the first mile of the Swale.* Follow it through a gate to cross a stone-arched bridge on the river. *This substantial, grassy surfaced structure bears a datestone of 1840.* Resume up the opposite bank, and after being deflected by trees up to a gate, advance straight on through a couple of gates to Firs.

Take a track left of the house to maintain your upstream course, initially enclosed. After opening out it runs to a gate then swings left to become enclosed on approaching Stone House: don't follow it but turn right up the firm access track. When it turns to climb away from the adjacent wall bear left, rising steadily above the wall on rough moor-grass to a stile just above the corner at the far end. From it rise half-right through dry reeds to the renovated cottage of Birkdale, and then follow its rough access track up to a gate. Once through, leave the track and rise gently left, avoiding excessive reedy areas to quickly join the unfenced B6270 road.

Go left a short way as far as a drive on the left. Making use of Open Access for a short while turn directly up the slopes above, a short stiff pull negotiating a low scarp to quickly ease out, then slanting right to a prominent cairn on scattered stones. This reveals lonely

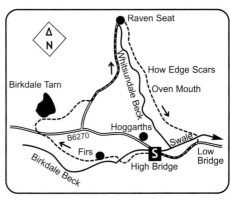

yet extensive Birkdale Tarn on its ledge ahead, a lovely moment. Advance less than a hundred yards to stand on its shore. *The low embankment dates from the lead mining days, when full use would have been made of this plentiful water supply. A complete surround of wild fell country features Nine Standards Rigg, Rogan's Seat, High Seat and Great Shunner Fell.*

Between the cairn and the tarn you crossed a grassy track: from the outflow of the tarn to your right rejoin that track to follow it left (east), away from the tarn. It rises to a small scattering of stones, just past which keep right on the main way, dropping gently and with the road visible further below. The track forges on, soon curving left on a neat shelf alongside reedy tussocks and beneath a heathery bank. This runs on to approach the scar of Hill Top Quarry, but neatly veers right before it to drop onto the unfenced Raven Seat road. Turn left past Hill Top along this peaceful access road to its terminus at Raven Seat.

Raven Seat is a tiny farming hamlet more than a little off the beaten track, but with refreshments often available in the left-hand dwelling. Enter by a stone-arched bridge, then turn right over another up to the front of the right-hand cottage. From a gate/stile on the right head downstream parallel with Whitsundale Beck. This is the first major tributary of the Swale, and offers an attractive waterfall in the second pasture, just past a sheepfold.

From a gate just beyond, a broad green path climbs left to a barn, then on a level course past further barns and gateways amid rough pastures. *During this section you gaze into the splendid wooded gorge of How Edge Scars.* After several level pastures with a wall for company you emerge through a last gate into a dramatic scene at Oven Mouth. *Here craggy and colourful slopes plunge with style to an ox-bow on Whitsundale Beck.* Advancing across open country the path soon forks: take the right one to pass along the bottom side of a large crumbling enclosure. With intermittent moist sections a guidepost beyond it points the way down to the barns of Smithy Holme ahead. Follow their firm access track left to a corner gate to drop past another abandoned farm. Passing an old limekiln the track crosses the Swale at Low Bridge to rejoin the B6270. Turn right for a steady few minutes along the road back to High Bridge. *The confluence of Whitsundale Beck with the Swale is seen to good advantage, as is a lovely little waterfall on the Swale.*

The Swale below Hoggarths

TAN HILL

START *Tan Hill   Grid ref. NY 897066*

DISTANCE *6 miles (9½km)*

ORDNANCE SURVEY MAPS
1:50,000
*Landranger 91 - Appleby-in-Westmorland **or***
Landranger 92 - Barnard Castle & Richmond
1:25,000
Explorer OL30 - Yorkshire Dales, North/Central

ACCESS *Start from the Tan Hill Inn. Roadside parking.*

A wild walk over varied moorland terrain, recommended in dry weather only: by contrast it concludes with a long road walk

At 1725ft/526m Tan Hill is the highest pub in the land. The apparently bleak moorlands all around are pitted with former coal mines which largely served lead smelting mills in Swaledale and Arkengarthdale. Minor but important roads meet here from Keld via Stonesdale, Reeth via Arkengarthdale and Stainmore via Barras. Tan Hill was a meeting place of drovers and packhorse ways, and today catches the passing trade of tourists, in summer at least: Pennine Wayfarers view the pub as a veritable oasis. Winters are a different matter, and harsh climate and enforced isolation have seen less resilient landlords survive only one before accepting defeat. Each May a sheep show draws farmers from many miles around. The place has found its way into the news at regular intervals: a double glazing advertisement and ensuing planning problems will be remembered by many; a wrangle over geographical identity featured a temporary transfer to Durham from its rightful county; while Tan Hill is now licensed to perform marriage ceremonies!

Leave by heading east on the road, over the cattle-grid. Just beyond, take a solid track on the right. This climbs to a relay booster station just above: you don't, however, but turn off it well before that along an inviting, embanked green track branching left at a right bend on the main track. Approaching a tiny fenced enclosure a thinner path forks off right through the heather. This remains thin but clear as it runs on through rougher heather, passing through a marshy section that is best circumvented to the right. Resuming, the path soon reaches the deep, intervening Mirk Fell Gill. Ideally locate the continuing path before heading off again, a thin way bearing right through further heather to a tiny ruin at the foot of the slope ahead. The thin path bears left above a small pool to a distinct grassy rake, an inviting track rising past a boundary stone and an old mineshaft protected by iron bars. *There are many old coal workings on these moors, not all of which are so obvious nor so well covered. It cost 5p to confirm this truly is a deep shaft. From here you can gaze across the Eden Valley to the northern fells of Lakeland, while across Stainmore is the massif of Mickle Fell.*

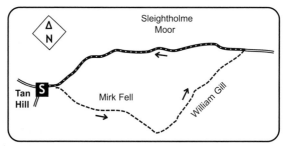

Just above the shaft the green rake falters, and an improving path rises more to the right through heather again. Marked by a string of cairns - the first as you level out - this runs unfailingly on and features some good grass sections in the heather of Mirk Fell. *Directly ahead is the rounded bulk of Water Crag, subsidiary of Rogan's Seat.* The path encounters a few peaty moments before descending, down over a minor gill and bearing more right again before dropping to the rim of the main watercourse hereabouts, William Gill. Dropping towards the beck, a thin path is met before the bottom. *That upstream is the continuing bridleway as it fords*

the beck and heads invitingly off. Your route however is the thin branch left, remaining on your side of the beck. This runs through moist reeds to quickly arrive at the scant remains of William Gill House, and more relevantly, the terminus of a shooters' track. Simply follow this downstream, a grand stride that crosses the beck several times during its course. *As three of the four crossings are concrete fords rather than bridges, in times of spate these can be a challenge.* As things open out, the track forks just short of the unseen road: keep left to rise to join the unfenced moor road from Reeth to Tan Hill - the walk's low point.

All that remains is to turn left and follow this open road back across the bleak moors, beginning with a prolonged climb. *Feel free to hitch a lift if desired, should anything come past! Before the brow you pass a rough road that crosses Sleightholme Moor for Bowes. Massive open views extend over miles of unkempt heather to Mickle Fell far beyond the waggons lumbering across Stainmore, while further right the valley of the Greta precedes Teesdale and its moors.* Your road rises further still to a brow, beyond which undulating strides lead to the Mirk Fell Culvert. *In 1948 this replaced a bridge of 1854 that is now buried in the embankment.* With the pub still out of sight the road begins another stiff pull, and by this stage you are probably cursing me. However, on the crest there comes the huge satisfaction of the 'mirage' finally appearing, and a well-earned pint is less than five minutes away!

Tan Hill Inn

WALK LOG

WALK	DATE	NOTES
1		
2		
3		
4		
5		
6		
7		
8		
9		
10		
11		
12		
13		
14		
15		
16		
17		
18		
19		
20		
21		
22		
23		
24		
25		

USEFUL ADDRESSES

Yorkshire Dales National Park
Hebden Road, Grassington, Skipton BD23 5LB • 01756-751600

Information Centres
National Park Centre, Hudson House **Reeth** DL11 6TE
• 01748-884059
Tourist Information, Friary Gardens, Victoria Rd **Richmond** DL10 4AJ
• 01748-850252

Yorkshire Dales Society
Town Hall, Settle BD24 9EJ • 01729-825600

Open Access
Helpline • 0845-100 3298 *or* www.countrysideaccess.gov.uk

Public Transport Information
Traveline • 0870 608 2608

In Gunnerside Gill

INDEX
walk number refers